"Daniel is a book for our day. The first half of Daniel shares multiple, encouraging examples that will help modern believers live faithfully for Christ in today's pagan, sinful culture. The last half of Daniel gives eschatological hope to all Christians who anticipate Christ's imminent return. Dr. Akin's exegesis of Daniel is precise in its explanation and practical in its application. I highly recommend this excellent work."

Steve Gaines, PhD, senior pastor, Bellevue Baptist Church, Memphis, past president of the Southern Baptist Convention

"This product of a scholar-pastor reflects the very best of each of these nomenclatures—both sound scholarship and heart-warming counsel and exposition of the text by a pastor who knows how to make the bridge from text to theology, exegesis to exhortation, and literary technicality to life-changing application."

Eugene H. Merrill, Distinguished Professor of Old Testament Studies Emeritus, Dallas Theological Seminary

"Danny Akin is one of the most gospel-focused, morally courageous, and exegetically skilled leaders in American Christianity. He lives up to his name as a Daniel who is willing to speak truth, no matter the cost. In this excellent commentary, you will be equipped to understand a biblical book that has proven confusing for many. Don't be intimidated away from the book of Daniel. This commentary will provide you with a clear, rich, gospel-resonant guide."

Russell Moore, director of the Public Theology Project at *Christianity Today*

"Daniel Akin's commentary on the book of Daniel is part of the Christ-Centered Exposition Commentary series that is designed to help pastors in their preparation to accurately proclaim the Word of God. In the commentary Akin outlines and explains the text of Daniel with a focus on exegetical accuracy. The outlines and divisions of each passage apply the Scriptural teaching to a contemporary modern audience with the aid of illustrations and theologically focused applications. At the end of each carefully examined chapter is a section on "How Does This Text Point to Christ?" or "Where Is Christ in This Text?" This is followed by challenging questions directed toward believers today based on the teaching of the passage.

"Being guided by the interpretive method that is found in the New Testament, Akin reads the Bible with an explicit messianic focus. The whole Bible must be read as Christian Scripture.

"This work is a model not only for the teaching of the book of Daniel but for the analysis of other books of the Bible as well. Pastors and teachers concerned about effectively proclaiming the book of Daniel (and other books of God's Word) will find this work to be an indispensable aid and model for proclaiming Scripture in our modern age."

Mark F. Rooker, senior professor of Old Testament and Hebrew, Southeastern Baptist Theological Seminary

"In a day of global political upheaval and rapidly changing cultural norms, God's people are facing incredible challenges to their faith. The lives of two Daniels intersect in this volume to show us how to navigate those challenges with integrity and godliness. One Daniel—a seasoned expositor and president—uncovers for us how the other Daniel—a saintly exile and prophet—held fast to the sovereignty of God amidst political opposition, religious persecution, and spiritual warfare. The result is an exegetically accurate and contemporarily relevant picture of living well as 'sojourners and exiles' in this world (cf. 1 Pet. 2:11). Read this book to help you see the glory of God's eternal kingdom and the Christ who reigns over it. Use it to learn how you and those you teach can live faithfully as strangers in this world as you wait for the next."

Jim Shaddix, D.Min, Ph.D., W. A. Criswell Professor of Expository Preaching, Southeastern Baptist Theological Seminary, Wake Forest, North Carolina

AUTHOR **Daniel L. Akin**

SERIES EDITORS **David Platt, Daniel L. Akin, and Tony Merida**

CHRIST-CENTERED

Exposition

EXALTING JESUS IN

DANIEL

HOLMAN®
REFERENCE
NASHVILLE, TENNESSEE

B&H Publishing Group
Nashville, Tennessee
All rights reserved.

ISBN: 978-0-8054-9687-1

Dewey Decimal Classification: 220.7
Subject Heading: BIBLE. O.T. DANIEL—
COMMENTARIES\JESUS CHRIST

Printed in the United States of America

5 6 7 8 9 10 • 26 25 24 23 22
BTH

SERIES DEDICATION

Dedicated to Adrian Rogers and John Piper. They have taught us to love the gospel of Jesus Christ, to preach the Bible as the inerrant Word of God, to pastor the church for which our Savior died, and to have a passion to see all nations gladly worship the Lamb.

—David Platt, Tony Merida, and Danny Akin
March 2013

AUTHOR'S DEDICATION

Dedicated to Daniel Lee, faithful pastor, preacher, evangelist, missionary, and visionary of Global Mission Baptist Church in Seoul, Korea. You are a blessing and inspiration to many.

—Danny Akin

ACKNOWLEDGMENTS

I am grateful for the wonderful assistance of Shane Shaddix, Mary Jo Haselton, and Kim Humphrey. This volume would not be possible without your invaluable assistance. Thank you for serving our Lord and me so well.

TABLE OF CONTENTS

SERIES INTRODUCTION

Augustine said, "Where Scripture speaks, God speaks." The editors of the Christ-Centered Exposition Commentary series believe that where God speaks, the pastor must speak. God speaks through his written Word. We must speak from that Word. We believe the Bible is God breathed, authoritative, inerrant, sufficient, understandable, necessary, and timeless. We also affirm that the Bible is a Christ-centered book; that is, it contains a unified story of redemptive history of which Jesus is the hero. Because of this Christ-centered trajectory that runs from Genesis 1 through Revelation 22, we believe the Bible has a corresponding global-missions thrust. From beginning to end, we see God's mission as one of making worshipers of Christ from every tribe and tongue worked out through this redemptive drama in Scripture. To that end we must preach the Word.

In addition to these distinct convictions, the Christ-Centered Exposition Commentary series has some distinguishing characteristics. First, this series seeks to display exegetical accuracy. What the Bible says is what we want to say. While not every volume in the series will be a verse-by-verse commentary, we nevertheless desire to handle the text carefully and explain it rightly. Those who teach and preach bear the heavy responsibility of saying what God has said in his Word and declaring what God has done in Christ. We desire to handle God's Word faithfully, knowing that we must give an account for how we have fulfilled this holy calling (Jas 3:1).

Second, the Christ-Centered Exposition Commentary series has pastors in view. While we hope others will read this series, such as parents, teachers, small-group leaders, and student ministers, we desire to provide a commentary busy pastors will use for weekly preparation of biblically faithful and gospel-saturated sermons. This series is not academic in nature. Our aim is to present a readable and pastoral style of commentary. We believe this aim will serve the church of the Lord Jesus Christ.

Third, we want the Christ-Centered Exposition Commentary series to be known for the inclusion of helpful illustrations and theologically driven applications. Many commentaries offer no help in illustrations, and few offer any kind of help in application. Often those that do offer illustrative material and application unfortunately give little serious attention to the text. While giving ourselves primarily to explanation, we also hope to serve readers by providing inspiring and illuminating illustrations coupled with timely and timeless application.

Finally, as the name suggests, the editors seek to exalt Jesus from every book of the Bible. In saying this, we are not commending wild allegory or fanciful typology. We certainly believe we must be constrained to the meaning intended by the divine Author himself, the Holy Spirit of God. However, we also believe the Bible has a messianic focus, and our hope is that the individual authors will exalt Christ from particular texts. Luke 24:25-27,44-47 and John 5:39,46 inform both our hermeneutics and our homiletics. Not every author will do this the same way or have the same degree of Christ-centered emphasis. That is fine with us. We believe faithful exposition that is Christ centered is not monolithic. We do believe, however, that we must read the whole Bible as Christian Scripture. Therefore, our aim is both to honor the historical particularity of each biblical passage and to highlight its intrinsic connection to the Redeemer.

The editors are indebted to the contributors of each volume. The reader will detect a unique style from each writer, and we celebrate these unique gifts and traits. While distinctive in their approaches, the authors share a common characteristic in that they are pastoral theologians. They love the church, and they regularly preach and teach God's Word to God's people. Further, many of these contributors are younger voices. We think these new, fresh voices can serve the church well, especially among a rising generation that has the task of proclaiming the Word of Christ and the Christ of the Word to the lost world.

We hope and pray this series will serve the body of Christ well in these ways until our Savior returns in glory. If it does, we will have succeeded in our assignment.

David Platt
Daniel L. Akin
Tony Merida
Series Editors
February 2013

Daniel

Be Strong and of Good Courage
(Preparing Our Children for the Nations)

DANIEL 1:1-21

Main Idea: Even in times of great trial and opposition, Christians must remain faithful to God and his gospel, imitating Christ's own steadfastness as he endured persecution and death for our sakes.

I. **God May Sovereignly Send You to a Difficult Place to Spread His Name among the Nations (1:1-3).**
   A. God works in spite of the sins of his people (1:1-2).
   B. God works as he scatters his people (1:3).

II. **Be Prepared for the Challenges Non-Christian Cultures Will Throw at You to Lead You Away from God (1:3-7).**
   A. Isolation (1:3)
   B. Indoctrination (1:4)
   C. Assimilation (1:5)
   D. Confusion (1:6-7)

III. **Determine Early in Your Life and Heart That You Will Not Compromise Your Convictions and Commitments to God (1:8-13).**
   A. Resist the temptation to defile yourself (1:8).
   B. Win the favor of those in authority when possible (1:9-10).
   C. Wisely offer alternative solutions that are win-win (1:11-13).

IV. **Trust God to Honor Your Devotion and Faithfulness to Him (1:14-21).**
   A. God blessed them physically (1:14-16).
   B. God blessed them mentally (1:17,20).
   C. God blessed them spiritually (1:17).
   D. God blessed them socially (1:18-21).

When we find our feet forcibly planted in the soil of an anti-God, anti-Christian culture, it is absolutely imperative that our hearts be drawn to heaven and our minds be immersed in the Word of God. As Paul wrote in Colossians 3:1-2, "So if you have been raised with Christ, seek the things above, where Christ is, seated at the right hand of God. Set your minds on things above, not on earthly things." As Paul adds in

Romans 12:2, "Do not be conformed to this age, but be transformed by the renewing of your mind." Thoughts like these were essential for four Hebrew teenagers who had been plucked from their families and their country and taken captive to the evil empire of that day, the empire of Babylon. Their names are Daniel, Hananiah, Mishael, and Azariah (1:6).

The theme of the book called Daniel is the sovereignty of God in all things. He is sovereign over the big things like international powers, and he is sovereign over small things like the apparently insignificant lives of teenagers. He is sovereign over history and is sovereign concerning the future. Our God is sovereign.

Though it is something of an oversimplification, the book can be divided into two parts: chapters 1–6 focus on the prophet (the man), and chapters 7–12 reveal the prophecies (the message), with Daniel as the central figure in both sections.

The contents of the book span a time period from about 605 through 539 BC. Using both narrative and apocalyptic vision, Daniel encourages God's people to trust in God's providence and remain faithful no matter what happens since their Lord is in complete control. Ronald Pierce highlights three specific themes that naturally flow out of this basic proposition: (1) God is able to rescue and reward faithful servants; (2) God holds accountable people and kings who oppose him; and (3) in the end God will replace all earthly kingdoms with his eternal kingdom (*Daniel*, 9).

My good friend and New Testament scholar, Bob Stein, once told me that among the persecuted believers around the world the two most favored books in the Bible are Daniel and Revelation. This is because both teach that in the end our God wins. The text before us, Daniel 1, reveals that God once won the day for four faithful Hebrew teens in a foreign and distant land away from family and friends. How did God do it? What was he up to?

God May Sovereignly Send You to a Difficult Place to Spread His Name among the Nations
DANIEL 1:1-3

Dale Davis well says, "Sometimes God may allow hardships to reach us because he wants his mercy to reach beyond us" (*Message of Daniel*, 36). God's purpose in such hardships is almost always multifaceted. He allows suffering in the lives of his people to demonstrate his sovereignty, strengthen their faith, show himself wise and strong, and put his glory on display among the nations that they might be drawn to him.

That there is pain for us in all of this is often the case. That there is great gain for the glory of God and the advance of his kingdom is certain. Such a perspective will help us remember who the true hero of Daniel is. It is not the Hebrew teenagers. It is a sovereign, all-powerful God of grace who, as Bryan Chapell notes,

> uses his sovereign power to maintain his covenant promises forever. This gospel according to Daniel should give us courage against our foes, hope in our distress, and perseverance in our trials. (*Gospel According to Daniel,* 9)

God Works in Spite of the Sins of His People (1:1-2)

Throughout history, armies have invaded nations with acts of aggression and war. The results have been tragic: land destroyed, property destroyed and confiscated, and POWs taken captive and sent away to foreign lands never to see family and friends again. This is what happened to Daniel and his friends. They were uprooted and replanted in the harsh and wicked soil of the Babylonian Empire. And surprisingly, it was God's doing. It was God's plan.

Verse 1 provides the historical context. Verse 2 provides the theological explanation (note vv. 2, 9, and 17). Judah, the southern kingdom, had been in political and spiritual decline for some time. During the reign of Jehoiakim (609–598 BC), one of Judah's worst kings who was nothing like his godly father Josiah, King Nebuchadnezzar of Babylon (605–562 BC) attacked Jerusalem in 605 BC. This happened because "the Lord handed King Jehoiakim of Judah over to him, along with some of the vessels from the house of God" (v. 2). The vessels of God, as trophies of war, were transported to Babylon and placed in the house of a pagan god in Babylon—probably Marduk, the chief god of the Babylonians. This was a way of saying, "Our god is better and stronger than your god." Daniel, on the other hand, says, "Not so!" The people of God have sinned, and the real God is judging them. In the process he is extending his presence among the nations. God is at work even through the sins of his people.

God Works as He Scatters His People (1:3)

There would be three deportations of the people of Israel to Babylon (605, 597, 586 BC). In Deuteronomy the Lord had warned his people that if they disobeyed him, curses would come on them (Deut 28:15). These curses would include military defeat (Deut 28:25) and deportation (Deut 28:64). In the book of Daniel, we see that God kept his word.

In addition to the temple vessels that were brought to "the land of Babylon," Nebuchadnezzar orders a man named Ashpenaz to deport members both "from the royal family and from the nobility." This was intended to strip the nation of its best and brightest, as verse 4 makes clear, and benefit Babylon by adding those gifted individuals to its own ranks. Unknown to the Babylonians, however, is the fact that God is working through this conquest. This is a divine invasion of enemy territory! The city of man is being invaded by the city of God, to draw from Augustine. Babylon (or Shinar in some translations), the land of ziggurats (cf. Gen 10:10 and the tower of Babylon in Gen 11), idols, and false gods, the city that opposes the true God, is now being infiltrated by the Lord's army. It is a small incursion to be sure, but one that will accomplish far more than anyone could imagine. The "times of the Gentiles" have started (Luke 21:24). Israel will be oppressed and her people scattered, but the nations will now have a witness among them to the one true and living God.

Be Prepared for the Challenges Non-Christian Cultures Will Throw at You to Lead You away from God

DANIEL 1:3-7

We all have what is called a "worldview," a particular way of looking at and seeing life and the world in which we live. It shapes both the way we think and the way we live. Here are a few definitions and descriptions of a worldview to guide us:

- A worldview is a comprehensive view of life through which we think, understand, and judge, and which determines our approach to life and meaning.
- "A worldview is that basic set of assumptions that gives meaning to one's thoughts. A worldview is the set of assumptions that

someone has about the way things are, about what things are, about why things are" (Bush, *Handbook*, 70).

- "A worldview is a set of presuppositions (assumptions which may be true, partially true or entirely false) which we hold (consciously or subconsciously, consistently or inconsistently) about the basic make-up of our world" (Sire, *Universe Next Door*, 17).
- "One's worldview is perhaps best reflected by one's answers to the 'ultimate questions of life': Who am I? Why am I here? Where am I going? What's it all about? Is there a god? How can I live and die happily? What are good and evil? [What would I be willing to die for?]" (Olthuis, *Worldviews*, 153–64).

Today we live in a post-Christian context with an increasingly non-Christian and secular worldview. There is pressure from every direction to force us to conform to the mind-set and the spirit of the age. This challenge is not new. Daniel and his three friends faced the same challenges in their day.

Isolation (1:3)

The first step in making Babylonians out of the four Hebrew teenagers (called "young men" in v. 4) was isolation from their homeland, family, and friends. This would have been traumatic and a shock to their systems, throwing their world into a tailspin. They would be extremely vulnerable, isolated, and separated from all that was familiar, making them far more susceptible to the "new ideas" they would encounter. This Babylonian strategy would increase the likelihood of their deconversion from their faith in the Lord God and their conversion to the worldview of Babylon.

I see this same strategy successfully employed by the evil one in our own day. However, in our case, it is often voluntary! Naively and sometimes willingly, parents send their children off to a secular college or university as lambs prepared for slaughter. Isolated from their church and Christian friends, they are quickly seduced by so-called intellectual elites and walk away from Christ. The evil one knows what he is doing! This does not mean parents should never send their children to secular or state universities. It does mean, though, that we fail to appreciate the danger and deception of false ideas if we do not adequately prepare students for that environment and support them while they are there.

Indoctrination (1:4)

Verse 4 affirms these four young men were among the best of the Israelites. In addition to coming "from the royal family and from the nobility" (v. 3), they were good-looking ("without any physical defect," probably indicating that they were not made eunuchs), they were smart ("suitable for instruction in all wisdom, knowledgeable, perceptive"), and they were blessed with leadership and interpersonal skills ("capable of serving in the king's palace"). They were ideal candidates to be taught "the Chaldean language and literature," to be enrolled in an educational indoctrination school "for three years" (vv. 4-5).

Brainwashing was to begin immediately in a world unlike anything they had ever known. The University of Babylon would give them a first-class secular education in Babylonian language, philosophy, literature, science, history, and astrology. Religion would have been a part of the curriculum as well as the mythologies of Babylon, the greatness of Marduk, and the importance of the pantheon of polytheistic deities that dominated the ancient Near Eastern world. Dream interpretation and omen reading would also be in their required course load. Looking at their education, we see that the New Age movement is not really that new. It is simply the Old Age wrapped up in a different package.

Assimilation (1:5)

Converting these followers of Yahweh into patriots of Babylon required a total immersion into the world of Babylon. While changing their minds, the Babylonians also sought to change the Hebrews' lifestyles. Each was to eat like a Babylonian and drink like a Babylonian. The goal was to entice them with the delicacies and privileges of their new life. Such an immersion would wear them down and eventually win them over. And at the end of three years, these boys would be given a final exam before the king.

Confusion (1:6-7)

In verses 6-7, we are introduced to four of the Hebrew aristocracy exiled to Babylon. Certainly there were others, but the book of Daniel records the story of only these four. Each was from the tribe of Judah. And as Ronald Pierce and others point out, the youths' Hebrew names honor the one true God, Yahweh. The name *Daniel* translates "Elohim is my

judge"; *Hananiah*, "Yahweh is gracious"; *Mishael*, "Who is like Elohim?";
and *Azariah*, "Yahweh helps" (Pierce, *Daniel*, 13).

Changing names today is not a big deal. In the ancient world,
however, it was huge. It went to the identity and core of who a person
was. The new names are familiar to most of us:

Old Name	New Name
Daniel	Belteshazzar
Hananiah	Shadrach
Mishael	Meshach
Azariah	Abednego

The exact meanings of these new Babylonian names is not certain,
though "certainly they were intended to honor Babylonian gods in
similar ways" to their Hebrew names (Pierce, *Daniel*, 13). And they were
intended to confuse these young men and reorient them away from
Yahweh and toward the pagan gods of their new home. Never was it
more important for these four teens to be in the world but not of the
world. But would they remain true to their faith? Could they? The rest
of the story provides our answer.

Determine Early in Your Life and Heart That You Will Not Compromise Your Convictions and Commitments to God
DANIEL 1:8-13

When I think of these four Hebrew teenagers, Psalms 1 and 2 immediately come to my mind. Psalm 1 depicts the character of the Messiah-
King. Psalm 2 promises his reign. Psalm 1 speaks of the man who is
not enticed and seduced by "the advice of the wicked" (v. 1). No, "his
delight is in the LORD's instruction" (v. 2). This accurately and beautifully describes Daniel and his friends. Having been raised and trained
by godly parents and grandparents, they loved the Lord their God
with their whole hearts, souls, minds, and strength (cf. Deut 6:4; Matt
22:37). They had been prepared, I have no doubt, by their parents and
spiritual mentors for this day, and they would be of good courage and
stand strong in the Lord!

Resist the Temptation to Defile Yourself (1:8)

"Daniel determined" begins verse 8. The immersion into the worldview of pagan Babylon would not win his heart or his mind. Babylon is where he would live, but Babylon would never be his home. Like his forefather Abraham, "he was looking forward to the city that has foundations, whose architect and builder is God" (Heb 11:10).

And exactly what did Daniel resolve to do? He resolved "that he would not defile himself with the king's food or with the wine he drank." The reason Daniel viewed the food and wine as defiling is not completely clear. It may have been dietary, if the food was unclean for a Hebrew (cf. Lev 11:1-23). It may have been religious or spiritual, if these items had been offered to idols (cf. Deut 6:13-15). It may have been symbolic: he would not pledge absolute loyalty to the king. Dale Davis proffers what he calls the defensive view, and personally I am drawn to it. He writes,

> Babylon was simply smothering Daniel and his friends. Daniel may well have thought, "There is real danger here: I could get sucked up into this and neutered by it all!" He recognized that if Babylon [the world and its values] gets into you, the show is over. (*Message of Daniel*, 32)

Daniel and his friends were forced to be in Babylon, but they would not let Babylon get into them. They made a conscious and determined decision to say no.

With courage and conviction Daniel approached the chief of the eunuchs and requested that he allow him to disregard the king's order and not defile himself. What amazing boys their parents had raised! The stand they were taking had been years in the making. It did not happen overnight.

Win the Favor of Those in Authority When Possible (1:9-10)

Daniel had more than conviction; he also had wisdom. He was blessed by God to walk in holiness and humility, a rare combination in any age. God honored his servant as a result. As "the Lord handed King Jehoiakim" into the hands of Nebuchadnezzar (v. 2), he "granted Daniel kindness [Hb *hesed*] and compassion from the chief eunuch." Daniel shared his faith and convictions with Ashpenaz, and it moved this unbelieving official. Daniel stood his ground, but he did so with grace and humility. He was not arrogant or rude. He was not obnoxious or stubborn. He kindly and winsomely won over his superior in this instance (cf. Joseph in Gen 39:4 and Esther in Esth 2:9).

Still, as impressed and sympathetic as Ashpenaz was with Daniel, he understandably feared the wrath of the king and the possibility of losing his head! If Daniel and his friends performed poorly on inspection day, it was probably not them but Ashpenaz who would suffer the most. He would be the one held responsible. Daniel had won the admiration and favor and concern of his pagan captor, but things appeared to be at an impasse.

Wisely Offer Alternative Solutions That Are Win-Win (1:11-13)

Daniel exhibits a wisdom far beyond his years, a wisdom that could have only come from God. It appears there are only two options. *Option 1:* They defile themselves. *Option 2:* Their new friend Ashpenaz loses his head. Daniel, however, proposes a third way, one in which everybody wins. He drops down the chain of command to the steward or "guard" (NIV) that Ashpenaz had assigned over them and proposes the following solution:

> *Please test your servants for ten days. Let us be given vegetables
> to eat and water to drink. Then examine our appearance and the
> appearance of the young men who are eating the king's food, and deal
> with your servants based on what you see.* (1:12–13)

The number ten may be either literal or symbolic, but the main point is that Daniel asks for a test—one that essentially puts his God to the test. He believes and trusts God to honor their convictions and commitments to obeying his Word.

Their diet would be simple, and it would not break Mosaic laws, would not have been offered to pagan gods, and would not unduly obligate the four Hebrews to the Babylonian king (Pierce, *Daniel*, 19). Chapell is right: "Holiness is risky business . . . society may praise idealism, but it rarely tolerates living those ideals" (*Gospel According to Daniel*, 17). Daniel knew that defilement would only further distance him from his Lord. He would risk it all to keep that from happening. The choice was worth it. I really appreciate Chuck Swindoll's summary of these verses:

> In a world filled with people who rebel against the divine King,
> it is inevitable that believers of all ages will face situations in

which their convictions will be challenged. We who are parents need to prepare our children for those occasions by both teaching them God's truth and modeling integrity. And all of us who are Christians need to personally commit ourselves to living God's way regardless of the temptations to live otherwise. (*God's Pattern for the Future,* 17)

This is what Daniel and his friends had been taught. This is how they would live or die.

Trust God to Honor Your Devotion and Faithfulness to Him
DANIEL 1:14–21

The great missionary to China, Hudson Taylor, said, "Unless there is the element of *extreme risk* in our exploits for God, there is no need for faith" (Newell, *Expect Great Things,* 89, emphasis added). There is little doubt that Daniel and his friends' exploits, fueled by faith that God would honor their devotion, had the element of extreme risk. Indeed, the risk potentially could involve the deaths of Ashpenaz, his steward, and Daniel and his friends. However, the Hebrews had settled in their hearts long ago that they would remain faithful to their God no matter what. *Compromise* was a word that was not in their vocabulary when it came to spiritual conviction and commitments. God honored this in an amazing way!

God Blessed Them Physically (1:14-16)

The steward of the chief eunuch listened to four Hebrews and allowed them to pursue this dietary test "for ten days," a definite and limited time (v. 14). The test was a resounding success, as God blessed them and rewarded their devotion to him. They "looked better and healthier than all the young men who were eating the king's food" (v. 15). *The Message* says, "They looked better and more robust than all the others." Daniel and his friends had resisted what the Reformer Heinrich Bullinger (1504–75) called the king's "sweet poison" (Olasky, "Dare to Be a Daniel," 64). The steward, as a result of their appearance and strength, "continued to remove their food and the wine they were to drink and gave them vegetables" (v. 16). Daniel and his friends had honored God, and God had honored them by giving them favor with the guard and healthy bodies. Tremper Longman summarizes it well:

[Daniel] proposes this time a brief ten-day test . . . the guard agrees; the test works; and the four eat vegetables to the glory of God for three years. (*Daniel*, 54)

God Blessed Them Mentally (1:17,20)

For the third time God gives (vv. 2,9). Here God gives the four youths "knowledge and understanding in every kind of literature and wisdom." Verse 20 informs us, "In every matter of wisdom and understanding that the king consulted them about, he found them ten times better than all the magicians and mediums in his entire kingdom." These four were "Proverbs men" with the ability to see the things of life and this world from God's perspective and to act accordingly. Again, there is striking irony in the situation.

> God gave the four Judeans "knowledge and understanding." Of course Nebuchadnezzar and those involved in their education would take the credit for their brilliance, but Daniel and the others would know to whom the credit was due. . . . For now, however, the divine origin of Daniel's success is only understood in private by the four. (Longman, *Daniel*, 54)

Today by the gift of God's divine revelation, we know the real story too.

God Blessed Them Spiritually (1:17)

God specifically blessed Daniel spiritually by giving him understanding in "visions and dreams of every kind." This gift from God would prove extremely valuable in chapter 2 and beyond (cf. 4:4-27; 5:11-31; 7:1–8:27; 9:20-27; 10:1–12:13).

John MacArthur notes,

> God enabled Daniel to interpret dreams and to receive visions. Visions and dreams were both a means of revelation from God, the former occurring while awake and the latter, while asleep. So Daniel was gifted as a seer, or prophet. As such, he was to serve as the very vehicle of God's divine revelations. This verse, then, becomes the backdrop for the rest of Daniel's prophecy. (*An Uncompromising Life*, 49)

God Blessed Them Socially (1:18-21)

After their three years of education, the four Hebrew teens are brought by the chief of the eunuchs to stand before the king, Nebuchadnezzar. They stood head and shoulders above all the rest: "No one was found equal to Daniel, Hananiah, Mishael, and Azariah." Therefore, "they began to attend the king" (v. 19). They were brought right into the palace and into the king's court; they were that impressive! Because they were socially, educationally, and personally superior—"ten times better than all the magicians and mediums in his entire kingdom"—Nebuchadnezzar gave the four Hebrews key administrative posts. He was confident they would serve and represent him well. Already in this Old Testament narrative we see the living out of that cardinal principle in Colossians 3:22-24:

> Slaves, obey your human masters in everything. Don't work only while being watched, as people-pleasers, but work wholeheartedly, fearing the Lord. Whatever you do, do it from the heart, as something done for the Lord and not for people, knowing that you will receive the reward of an inheritance from the Lord. You serve the Lord Christ.

We see them embodying Paul's exhortation, "Whether you eat or drink, or whatever you do, do everything for the glory of God" (1 Cor 10:31).

Verse 21 is not so much a footnote as it is a summary of the long life and ministry of Daniel. Stephen Miller speculates that he lived eighty-five or ninety years (ca. 620–535 BC), noting that

> Daniel lived through the entire Neo-Babylonian period (the exile) and continued into the reign of Cyrus (when the Jews were released from captivity), thus outliving his Babylonian captors. (*Daniel*, 73–74)

John MacArthur notes just how far the influence of the exiled teen possibly extended before it came to an end:

> Daniel served in his influential position for seventy years. His integrity and uncompromising character had far-reaching results, for when I see the wise men coming from the East, I think of the impact Daniel's theology must have had upon the Chaldeans' astrology. God gave him the influence that I believe led to the decree of Cyrus to send the people back to their land . . . influence that led to the rebuilding of the wall

under Nehemiah and to the reestablishing of the nation of
Israel . . . influence that eventually led the wise men to come
to crown the King who was born in Bethlehem. Daniel was
behind the scenes of the history of the Messiah as well as the
Messiah's people. Daniel had unlimited influence for through
his prophecy he brings homage to the one who is the "KING
OF KINGS, AND LORD OF LORDS" (Rev. 19:16) who reigns
forever. (*An Uncompromising Life*, 50)

Conclusion: How Does This Text Point to Christ?

Daniel and his three companions remained faithful to their true identity, obeyed God, and were a shining testimony and witness both to God's
providence and to his grace. He sent them on a missionary journey,
making them leave all that was familiar so that they might bear a faithful and true witness to kings and nations in foreign lands. They beautifully typify another Hebrew who will arrive six hundred years later who
was also sent to a foreign land to bear witness to the one true God—a
Jew by the name of Jesus. Like Daniel and his friends, the Son of God
would leave his home and willingly embrace a sinful world without defiling himself even once (2 Cor 5:21; Heb 4:15; 1 Pet 2:21-25). Like these
Hebrew boys he "would find favor with God and man (Luke 2:40 and
52). When he was still a child, his teachers 'were amazed at his understanding and his answers' (Luke 2:47)" (Helm, *Daniel for You*, 28). Jesus
is the embodiment of the wisdom of God (1 Cor 1:30).

Christ is the greater Daniel, the greater Hannaniah, the greater
Mishael, and the greater Azariah. Jesus refused to compromise when
he faced the emperor behind the emperor—Satan. How did Satan
tempt Jesus to defile himself? He did so with food! Yet Christ remained
faithful. Christ took the judgment faithless Israel deserved at the hands
of another pagan empire, but he walked away from death to outlast the
Roman Empire and every empire to come.

There is a certain divine irony in all this that is hard to miss. It is
grace filled and gospel rich. Daniel, Hananiah, Mishael, and Azariah
will give a faithful witness before Ashpenaz and Nebuchadnezzar and
be brought to live in the king's palace. Jesus, in contrast, would give a
faithful witness before Herod and Pilate and be nailed to a cross. And yet
by his death all who trust him will live forever with the King of kings and
Lord of lords in his eternal palace. So be strong and of good courage in

whatever God calls you to do. He is with you, and he is accomplishing so much more than meets the eye!

Reflect and Discuss

1. In what ways do you see the sovereignty of God on the big stage of world history? In what ways do you see his sovereignty in your own life?
2. Why do you suppose persecuted Christians gravitate toward Daniel and Revelation? How do these books of prophecy inform our present living?
3. In the story of Daniel, God is working even through the sins of his people. Where else in Scripture can we see God work despite or even through great sin?
4. Compare and contrast the scattering of God's people in Daniel 1 with that of Acts 8. How does God use each of these scenarios?
5. Think about your own worldview. What beliefs or assumptions characterize how you view the world? Now think about your culture as a whole. What characterizes the general culture's worldview?
6. How have you experienced the challenges of isolation, indoctrination, assimilation, and confusion? How did you fight to remain faithful to Christ?
7. What does it mean to be defiled by the world? What defensive measures can you take to protect against being defiled? Is it possible to be too protective? Explain.
8. Why does the presence of risk require faith in Christ? Because you identified with Christ, have you ever experienced risk that required deep faith? If so, explain.
9. What physical, mental, and spiritual blessings has the Lord given to you? How can you use them to bring glory and honor to him the way Daniel and his friends did?
10. How does Daniel's journey mirror the life and ministry of Jesus? How does Jesus fulfill the work done by Daniel?

God's Kingdom: The Only Kingdom That Will Never Be Destroyed

DANIEL 2:1-49

Main Idea: God sovereignly works to reveal his greatness and his coming kingdom in Christ so that all peoples will praise and worship him.

I. **God Creates Impossible Situations to Reveal His Greatness (2:1-16).**
    A. Unbelievers may respond with threats and anger (2:1-13).
    B. Believers should respond with wisdom and faith (2:14-16).
II. **God Delights in the Prayers and Praise of His Children (2:17-23).**
    A. Go to God in prayer (2:17-19).
    B. Respond to God's goodness with praise (2:19-23).
III. **God Reveals the Mystery of His Kingdom to Demonstrate His Power (2:24-45).**
    A. Only the God of heaven knows all things (2:24-30).
    B. Only the God of heaven can do all things (2:31-45).
        1. God revealed the content of the dreams (2:31-35).
        2. God provided the interpretation of the dreams (2:36-45).
            a. Babylon is the head of gold.
            b. Medo-Persia is the chest and arms of silver.
            c. Greece is the stomach and thighs of bronze.
            d. Rome is the legs of iron with feet of iron and clay.
            e. The stone that smashes and becomes a great mountain is Christ and the kingdom of God.
IV. **God Honors His Servants Who Faithfully Serve Him (2:46-49).**
    A. God may choose to have people praise them (2:46-47).
    B. God may choose to have people promote them (2:48-49).

Man, with his ambitions, ego, and idolatries, is often impressed by what he can build. God, on the other hand, is not dazzled by man's accomplishments. If you would like God's opinion on the great kingdoms men build in this world, then look at Daniel 2:35, where he says they all "were shattered and became like chaff from the summer threshing floors. The wind carried them away, and not a trace of them could be found." In our modern vernacular we might say they are dust in the wind. They are here today and gone tomorrow. Only one kingdom "will never be destroyed." It is the kingdom "the God of the heavens will set up" (v. 44), the kingdom God revealed in dreams to a pagan king named Nebuchadnezzar, dreams that only his servant Daniel could interpret.

In Daniel 1:17 we are told that God gave Daniel understanding in "visions and dreams of every kind." Now in chapter 2 we see how valuable this gift from God is. It is a gift that will save not only Daniel's life but also the lives of his friends (see v. 17) and the lives of all the wise men, magicians, enchanters, astrologers, and sorcerers in Babylon. How did all of this come to pass?

God Creates Impossible Situations to Reveal His Greatness
DANIEL 2:1-16

Daniel 2–7 has a number of interesting characteristics that enhance our understanding of what God is trying to teach us. First, there is an obvious parallelism or chiastic structure, which looks something like this:

A—Dream about four earthly kingdoms and God's kingdom
    (ch. 2)
    B—Story about Jews being faithful in the face of death
        (ch. 3)
        C—Story about royal hubris that is humbled (ch. 4)
        C´—Story about royal hubris that is humbled (ch. 5)
    B´—Story about a Jew who is faithful in the face of death
        (ch. 6)
A´—Vision about four earthly kingdoms and God's kingdom
    (ch. 7)
(Lucas, *Daniel*, 68; Hill, "Daniel," 57)

Second, 2:4–7:28 is written not in Hebrew but in Aramaic. The shift to Aramaic has long puzzled scholars with no consensus being reached. Andrew Hill provides a reasonable possibility when he writes,

> It would be only logical for the wise men to communicate with
> a language common to all, since the wise men are a racially
> and ethnically diverse group. ("Daniel," 60)

If Hill is correct, there is a missional impulse that must not go unnoticed in chapters 2–7. God's impossible situation is intended to reveal his greatness to the Gentile nations.

Unbelievers May Respond with Threats and Anger (2:1-13)

Nebuchadnezzar, Babylon's greatest and longest reigning king, had a series of bad dreams in the second year of his reign (604–603 BC). In fact, the dreams "troubled him, and sleep deserted him" (v. 1). In the ancient world dreams were regarded as significant. They were often viewed as predictions of future events. When it was the dream of a king, his kingdom's future could be in view; and if he understood its meaning, he could take action and make preparation for what was on the horizon. So like any monarch Nebuchadnezzar sought the counsel of his wise men to help him interpret and understand his dreams (vv. 2-3). Eager to serve their king, they say, "Tell your servants the dream, and we will give the interpretation" (v. 4).

In verse 5, however, the king throws a horrifying curveball to the wise men. He wanted his college of counselors to tell him both the dream and its interpretation. If they don't, or if they can't, they will be dismembered, and their houses will be turned into a garbage dump (v. 5). Body parts, outhouses, and dunghills are in their immediate future unless they obey his command because, "My word is final." On the other hand, if they do their job, they will receive gifts, a reward, and great honor (v. 6).

Not knowing what to do, the wise men ignore what Nebuchadnezzar said and repeat their request for the king to tell them the dream (v. 7). This turns out to be a bad move, as it ticks the king off, and he accuses them of stall tactics and conspiracy (vv. 8-9). The wise men (repeatedly called "the Chaldeans") respond and accuse the king of making an utterly unreasonable request (vv. 10-11). In fact, only "the gods, whose dwelling is not with mortals" could pull off this feat (cf. Isa 46:9-10). Ironically, they got this one just about right, but it did not help them one bit with the king.

Verse 12 informs us the king became violently angry (ESV, "angry and very furious") and gave orders to execute all the wise men of Babylon. Things have gone from bad to worse for this group that we now learn, in verse 13, includes Daniel and his friends. Apparently they had not been among the others who failed at Nebuchadnezzar's request. Still, guilt by association condemns them. All are to be executed by the decree of this volatile and unreasonable pagan king. What a contrast he is to Daniel, as we are about to see!

Believers Should Respond with Wisdom and Faith (2:14-16)

Arioch, the head of Nebuchadnezzar's execution squad, comes looking for Daniel and his friends to have them ripped to pieces. However, unlike the tempestuous king, Daniel is skillful "in all wisdom, knowledgeable, perceptive, and capable of serving in the king's palace" (1:4). God gave him favor and compassion before Ashpenaz in 1:9, and he does the same before Arioch in 2:14. Daniel responds "with tact and discretion" to "the captain of the king's guard" who was there to lead them to their execution. He wisely and respectfully raises a question: Why is the king so urgent in his decree to commit the mass murder of his major advisers (v. 15)? Arioch tells him why, and Daniel responds with an incredible act of courage and faith. He goes into the king's throne room and asks for time, the very thing Nebuchadnezzar said no to in verse 8. Trusting in his God, Daniel promises to return and "give the king the interpretation" (v. 16). Wow! Daniel is still a teenager, exiled, conquered, a slave, a man marked for death. Still he is calm, poised, and "fully capable of speaking truth to power" (Helm, *Daniel for You*, 32). The man of faith confronts the head of state. The question is, Will his God come through?

God Delights in the Prayers and Praise of His Children
DANIEL 2:17-23

Dee Duke wisely notes,

> Almost everyone believes that prayer is important. But there is a difference between believing that prayer is important and believing it is essential. "Essential" means there are things that will not happen without prayer. (Newell, *Expect Great Things*, 225)

The lives of Daniel, his friends, and all the wise men of Babylon are at stake. The request of the king is an impossible one to obey without divine intervention. Either God acts or they are finished—game over! What Daniel does when faced with such an impossible situation is exemplary: Pray → get some rest → praise!

Go to God in Prayer (2:17-19)

Amos 3:7 says, "Indeed, the Lord GOD does nothing without revealing his counsel to his servants the prophets." I think Daniel believed
this. He returned home "and told his friends Hananiah, Mishael, and
Azariah about the matter" (2:17). They then decided to do the only
thing they could, given the situation: they decided that they should "ask
the God of the heavens for mercy concerning this mystery" in prayer
that he might reveal the king's dream and spare their lives as well as the
lives of "the rest of Babylon's wise men" (v. 18; cf. v. 24). Daniel's concern for the welfare of the lost and pagan wise men of Babylon should
not go unnoticed. His heart for others is an example to us all. His obedience to Leviticus 19:18 sets the standard we should all attempt to reach.
Daniel then does a remarkable, mind-blowing thing: he goes to sleep!
He prayed, put the matter in God's hand, and did what the king could
not do (cf. v. 1). He got a good night's rest, and as he did, God revealed
the mystery "in a vision at night" (v. 19).

Respond to God's Goodness with Praise (2:19-23)

Songs that blend theology and worship permeate the Bible and not just
in the book of Psalms. The Old Testament includes the Song of the Sea
(Exod 15), Deborah's Song (Judg 5), Hannah's Song (1 Sam 2:1-10),
and the prayers of Jonah (Jonah 2) and Habakkuk (Hab 3). In the New
Testament there are Mary's Song, called the Magnificat (Luke 1:46-55),
Paul's hymns (e.g., Phil 2:5-11; 1 Tim 3:16), and the many songs in the
book of Revelation (e.g., 4:11; 5:9-10,12,13; 15:3-4; 19:1-2,5,7-8) (Fyall,
Daniel, 35). Daniel responds to God's answer to prayer with his own
theologically rich song of praise. Two ideas stand out. First, God is absolutely sovereign. Second, God alone gives revelation. This is the center
of chapter 2 and the place where Daniel wants us to focus. Interpreting
the dream is important, but knowing and worshiping God is ultimate.

"Daniel praised the God of the heavens," verse 19 tells us. "God
of the heavens" is an important title in chapter 2, appearing five times
(2:18,19,28,37,44). Its use is an important polemic against the pantheon
of Babylonian gods. Bob Fyall points out the significance of it in Daniel's
context:

> Not by horoscopes, séances and divination would
> enlightenment come, but from the God of heaven, a title also
> used in the post-Exilic books of Ezra and Nehemiah. This is

not simply the tribal God of Israel but the God who rules the heavenly bodies, of which the study and attempt to manipulate lay at the heart of Babylonian religion. (*Daniel*, 34)

What are the specifics of this theologically rich song? Daniel acknowledges seven aspects of God's character and activity. Specifically, he praises God for his eternality (v. 20); his omniscience and omnipotence (v. 20); his sovereignty over the nations (v. 21); his gifts of wisdom, knowledge, and understanding (v. 21); his revelation and knowledge (v. 22); his faithfulness to his people (v. 23); and for answering Daniel's prayer (v. 23). In light of this magnificent picture of God's goodness and greatness, we can exclaim with Daniel and all our brothers and sisters, "For the LORD is great and is highly praised; he is feared above all gods. For all the gods of the peoples are idols, but the LORD made the heavens" (Ps 96:4-5).

God Reveals the Mystery of His Kingdom to Demonstrate His Power
DANIEL 2:24-45

Daniel had used no astrology or board games to discover the content and meaning of the king's dream. He had consulted no dream manuals or read any livers, as other ancient diviners did to communicate with their useless and lifeless gods (Pierce, *Daniel*, 37). He went to the only God who truly exists, sought his mercy (v. 18), and got his answer. Like Joseph before Pharaoh in Genesis 40–41, a Hebrew slave by divine enablement will reveal God's plan and purposes to the man of power— power he possesses only by virtue of God's sovereign plan. Drama has been building. The narrator drew out the action to build suspense (Davis, *Message of Daniel*, 45). Now it's showtime!

Only the God of Heaven Knows All Things (2:24-30)

Daniel goes to Arioch, the executioner, and tells him not to kill anyone. Instead, he should take Daniel to the king, "and I will give him the interpretation" (v. 24). His class in biblical dream hermeneutics had paid off.

Arioch quickly (ESV, "in haste") brought Daniel to Nebuchadnezzar, appearing to take some credit ("I have found") for locating this Jewish slave who can solve the king's problem. The king asked Daniel, also called Belteshazzar, if he could indeed tell and interpret the dream. Daniel's answer is striking both in its honesty and in its humility, something from which we can all learn. He says, "No wise man, medium, magician, or diviner" can help you out (v. 27). To be blunt, they are impotent. On the other hand, "There is a God in heaven who reveals mysteries, and he has let King Nebuchadnezzar know what will happen in the last days" (v. 28; NIV, "days to come"). Daniel even details how and where God gave Nebuchadnezzar his dream (vv. 28-29)!

In addition to being able to reveal and interpret the dream, Daniel does another remarkable thing—the thing God's man should always do. He gives all the credit to God. Daniel's success comes not because he has more wisdom than anyone living. (I am not smarter, wiser, or more brilliant than others, Daniel admits.) Rather, this is all God's doing "in order that the interpretation might be made known to the king, and that you may understand the thoughts of your mind" (v. 30). I love what Sinclair Ferguson says at this point:

> This is the spirit of Jesus before the high priests and Pilate; it is the spirit of Elijah before Jezebel; it is the spirit of John the Baptist before Herod. Daniel is full of the spirit of truth. Even Nebuchadnezzar can recognize that. (*Daniel,* 52)

Only the God of Heaven Can Do All Things (2:31-45)

Verses 31-45 finally reveal the content and interpretation of the dream. They reveal a God who is absolutely sovereign in what he knows (omniscience) and what he will do (omnipotence). This God knows the future, has a plan for the future, and will accomplish that future. This is the God of Isaiah 46:9-10, where the Bible says,

> *Remember what happened long ago, for I am God, and there is no other; I am God, and no one is like me. I declare the end from the beginning, and from long ago what is not yet done, saying: my plan will take place, and I will do all my will.*

Making this practical and applicable to us today, David Jeremiah says, "You may not know what the future holds, but you know who holds the future. Since the whole world is in God's hands, your world is in God's hand" (*Agents of Babylon,* 52–53).

God revealed the content of the dreams (2:31-35). God showed the king a great image or statue that was powerful and bright (NIV, "dazzling") and frightening (NIV, "awesome") in appearance (v. 31). Its appearance was fourfold: (1) a head of gold, (2) chest and arms of silver, (3) stomach and thighs of bronze (v. 32), and (4) legs of iron with feet "partly iron and partly fired clay" (v. 33). However, something happens to the statue: "A stone broke off without a hand touching it [a divine stone!], struck the statue on its feet of iron and fired clay, and crushed them" (v. 34). Then the whole statue or image crumbled "and became like chaff from the summer threshing floors." Gone. Disappeared. "Not a trace of them could be found." In stark contrast, "the stone that struck the statue became a great mountain and filled the whole earth" (v. 35). This is the dream God gave the Babylonian king.

God provided the interpretation of the dreams (2:36-45). Daniel, by God's enablement, has told the king his dream. Now, by that same divine power, he gives its interpretation (v. 36). The beginning of his explanation is plain (vv. 37-38). The rest is more vague until the end (vv. 39-43,44-45). Still, most evangelical scholars who believe in predictive prophecy agree on what the various parts of the statue represent.

Babylon is the head of gold (2:37-38; cf. 2:32). Daniel tells Nebuchadnezzar his exalted status as king of the vast empire at that time was a divine gift. The language, which recalls the authority and dominion that God gave Adam in the garden of Eden (Gen 1:28-30), emphasizes the magnitude and magnificence of Babylon under Nebuchadnezzar (2:37-38). He is the head of gold, the representative of this awesome empire. However, he would be followed by a succession of weak and incompetent rulers. The great Babylonian kingdom would only last a mere sixty-five years (605–539 BC). This mighty empire came to an end in a hurry. Daniel 5 records its demise at the hand of Darius the Mede (probably another name for Cyrus).

Medo-Persia is the chest and arms of silver (2:39; cf. 2:32). Medo-Persia would follow Babylon in 539. It was inferior in its totalitarian rule. However, it would also be a vast empire and last for more than two hundred years (539–331 BC).

Greece is the stomach and thighs of bronze (2:39; cf. 2:32). The middle section of the body and the thighs of bronze, "which will rule the whole earth," represented Greece, built by Alexander the Great. He would conquer the known world and then die at the young age of thirty-three (356–323 BC). This kingdom would last for 185 years (331–146 BC).

Rome is the legs of iron with feet of iron and clay (2:40-43; cf. 2:33). The fourth kingdom is mighty Rome, a great and powerful empire that was "strong as iron," because "iron crushes and shatters everything, and like iron that smashes, it will crush and smash all the others" (v. 40). Rome, of course, is the greatest of history's empires. It lasted by some accounts and in some form from 146 BC to AD 1476 in the West and AD 1453 in the East. Sixteen hundred years later, its influence is still with us today, especially in Western civilization.

Verses 41-43 are vague and their meaning is uncertain, which calls for great humility by interpreters of this apocalyptic vision. Good, faithful students of the Bible are all over the place in how best to understand them. Following the insights of Stephen Miller, in part, I think we can at least make the following observations (*Daniel*, 98). First, Rome will be incredibly strong but also vulnerable and unstable, with numerous nations and divisions making up its empire (vv. 41-42). Historically, this was the case. Second, although various people groups and nations constitute the one Roman Empire, their unity was a tenuous and imposed unity. They are mixed in their union—not really one—and eventually they "will not hold together." This is true whether you date the dissolution of Rome at AD 395, 476, 1054, 1453, or 1476. The Roman Empire is gone. Whether it will be revived in the last days as a part of the empire led by the one the Bible calls the antichrist or the beast is a good and interesting question, but it is best addressed in other texts of Scripture.

The Stone that smashes and becomes a great mountain is Christ and the kingdom of God (2:44-45; cf. 2:34-36). These verses show us where the dream is pointing all along. Some understand the verses as pointing to the end of the age, when Christ comes again to establish his universal and visible kingdom (see Rev 19:11–20:6). Others believe they are pointing to his first coming and the inauguration of his kingdom. I believe both are in view (cf. Isa 61:1-2). They are pointing to his first coming and the inauguration of his kingdom, while also looking to and anticipating his eschatological kingdom. Like twin peaks with a hidden valley between, the kingdom is inaugurated at Christ's first coming and fully realized at his second. Old Testament prophecy often functions in this way.

In contrast to the temporal and chaff-like kingdoms of this world (cf. Ps 1:4-5), "the God of the heavens will set up a kingdom [by his Messiah, see Dan 7] that will never be destroyed" nor be given or left to another people or empire (v. 44). In fact, the kingdom of God "will crush all these kingdoms and bring them to an end." God's kingdom will "endure forever" (v. 44). He will do this by the stone that broke "off from the mountain without a hand touching it," a stone that will break and shatter and scatter like chaff "the iron, bronze, fired clay, silver, and gold." That this language of breaking and shattering recalls the language of the messianic Psalm 2 is not accidental or coincidental, for as we will see at the end, this stone is Christ! His kingdom is coming, and it will never end.

Daniel brings his interpretation to a close with two resounding affirmations: (1) a great God has revealed this, and (2) "the dream is certain, and its interpretation reliable" (v. 45). You can count on it! You can take it to the bank.

The *ESV Study Bible* provides a helpful note in summarizing the significance of the vision of this great image God gave King Nebuchadnezzar:

> Another point being made in the dream is that each earthly kingdom has its own glory but also its own end: both have been assigned to it by God. The progression of world history is typically not upward to glory and unity but rather downward to dishonor and disunity. Thus the statue progresses from gold, to silver, to bronze, to iron, and from one head, to a chest and arms, to a belly and thighs, to feet and toes of composite iron and clay. (This list of metals shows a progressive decrease in the value and splendor of the materials but an increase in toughness and endurance.) Some commentators understand this to indicate a general decline in the moral quality of the governments and an increase in the amount of time they lasted. In contrast, God's kingdom grows from humble beginnings to ultimate, united glory as a single kingdom that fills the whole earth forever. The stone that will break in pieces all these other four kingdoms is most likely Christ (see Luke 20:18). He is the mystery of the ages, the one in whom God plans to unite all things in his glorious kingdom (Eph. 1:9-10).[1]

God Honors His Servants Who Faithfully Serve Him
DANIEL 2:46-49

In the Sermon on the Mount (Matt 5–7), Jesus said,

> *You are the light of the world. A city situated on a hill cannot be hidden. No one lights a lamp and puts it under a basket, but rather*

---

[1] *The Holy Bible: English Standard Version: The ESV Study Bible* (Wheaton, IL: Crossway Bibles, 2008), 1590.

on a lampstand, and it gives light for all who are in the house. In the same way, let your light shine before others, so that they may see your good works and give glory to your Father in heaven. (Matt 5:14-16)

Daniel and his friends were indeed lights brightly shining in a dark place. Nebuchadnezzar could not deny the good works he saw in them. And even as a pagan king, he gave glory to the "God of gods," the Father of Daniel, Hananiah, Mishael, and Azariah.

God May Choose to Have People Praise Them (2:46-47)

The king acted in an unusual if not unprecedented manner: he fell face-down and "worshiped Daniel" (cf. Isa 49:7,23). Further, he "gave orders to present an offering and incense to him" (2:46). Nebuchadnezzar treats Daniel, I believe, as a representative of his God (Lucas, *Daniel,* 77). Tremper Longman is right: "Daniel is honored because of what his God has done, not because of what he has done" (*Daniel,* 83). This is confirmed by the confession (though not a confession of conversion) of the king in verse 47: "Your God is indeed God of gods, Lord of kings, and a revealer of mysteries, since you were able to reveal this mystery." David Helms's observation is helpful at this point:

> Daniel's God now shares the stage with the Babylonians'
> deities. Given what we know of Nebuchadnezzar's religiosity,
> this is truly amazing. The one who had been named for
> Babylon's deity of wisdom, who prayed to Marduk at his
> coronation only one year previously, now gave space to a
> competing deity and even offered public words of praise to
> him. For the first time in Nebuchadnezzar's life, Marduk had
> competition in his interior world—all because one godly
> man remained poised, prayerful and willing to speak truth to
> power. (*Daniel for You,* 42)

God May Choose to Have People Promote Them (2:48-49)

The king kept his word from verse 6 to give gifts and rewards and great honor to anyone who could cure his insomnia and make "the dream and its interpretation known." In the process life improved dramatically for Daniel and his friends. Daniel received a promotion "and many generous gifts." He became "ruler over the entire province of Babylon and chief governor over all the wise men of Babylon" (v. 48). Any way you slice it, this is impressive, and it was all the doing of Daniel's God!

Daniel did not forget his friends. He asked the king to appoint them to positions of authority and significance, and he did (v. 49). Theirs was a high honor, too, but it would also be a dangerous and risky position. Those at the top are easy targets. The trio will find this out in chapter 3. Daniel will find it out in chapter 6.

Conclusion: How Does Our Text Point to Christ?

That Daniel in this chapter is a foreshadowing of Jesus is easy to see. As David Helm points out,

> God took a conquered Hebrew prisoner of war, and stood him confidently before the ruler and his own execution—a foretaste of what Jesus would later do for us, except that he not only faced but endured execution. (*Daniel for You*, 35)

However, the image of "the stone that struck the statue [and] became a great mountain and filled the whole earth" (v. 35) should captivate our attention. The rock or stone imagery is rich and multifaceted in the Bible. Jesus is the Christ, the Son of the living God, the rock on which he builds his church and his kingdom (Matt 16:18). Psalm 118:22 speaks of a "stone that the builders rejected," which "has become the cornerstone." Matthew 21:42; Mark 12:10-11; Luke 20:17; and 1 Peter 2:7 all tell us the stone is Christ. Further, Isaiah 8:14 and 28:16 also use the stone imagery; and Romans 9:33 and 1 Peter 2:6 and 8 again cite these texts as pointing to Christ. But as Tremper Longman points out, we get a clear reference to Daniel 2 in Luke 20:18 (*Daniel*, 92–93). There Jesus quotes Psalm 118:22 and makes a direct connection to Daniel 2! The stone the builders rejected, which has become the cornerstone, is the stone that breaks and crushes everyone who falls on (i.e., rejects) that stone. Placing all of this in an end-time, eschatological context, Chuck Swindoll says it like this:

> When Jesus Christ returns to earth to establish His Millennial Kingdom, He will "break [the nations] with a rod of iron. [He will] shatter them like earthenware" (Ps. 2:9). As the smiting stone in Nebuchadnezzar's dream, the Lord will not absorb, restructure, or adapt to previous kingdoms; He will totally annihilate them and set up His own monarchy, which will be absolutely perfect politically, morally, economically, and

religiously. And He will rule over all the earth as King of kings and Lord of lords (Isa. 2:2-4; cf. Rev. 19:11-16). (*Daniel*, 27)

Christ is the stone the world rejected. He is the stone God will exalt and use to build his kingdom, one that will never be destroyed.

Reflect and Discuss

1. Think of a time you've faced or seen a seemingly impossible situation. How might God have used that situation to reveal his greatness?
2. What are some of the incorrect ways we often respond to difficult situations? Read Luke 6:43-45 and talk about what these responses reveal.
3. What does Daniel's response reveal about his faith and character? Did Daniel doubt God? Explain your answer.
4. What role does prayer play in your response to difficult situations? Do you tend to rely on God or ignore him and deal with the situation yourself? Explain your reasoning.
5. How do God's omniscience and omnipotence shape how Christians view the future?
6. Discuss how the stone from Nebuchadnezzar's dream may be about both Christ's first and second comings.
7. How should you respond when someone praises you for something God has done?
8. Why does God sometimes put his servants in places of high authority? What privileges come with such positions? What dangers?
9. In what ways does Daniel represent Christ in this passage?
10. What does the rock imagery of Scripture teach us about the character and work of Christ?

Courage in the Fire!

DANIEL 3:1-30

Main Idea: Because of the presence of God with us and Christ's work for us, believers can have courage to resist false gods and testify to the one true God.

I.   God's People Will Be Confronted with the Idols of This World (3:1-7).
II. God's People Will Be Criticized by the People of This World (3:8-12).
III. God's People Will Be Challenged to Worship the Gods of This World (3:13-15).
IV. God's People Must Be Courageous in the Face of Danger in This World (3:16-18).
V.   God's People Can Be Confident the Lord Is with Them No Matter What Happens in This World (3:19-30).

In Philippians 1:21 Paul writes, "For me, to live is Christ and to die is gain." John Piper calls this the ultimate win-win scenario. If I live, I get Christ. If I die, I get more of Christ! Either way I win! This way of thinking of life as walking with God and death as ushering one into God's presence must have been in the minds of three Hebrew men by the names of Hananiah, Mishael, and Azariah. We know these men, taken captive to Babylon in 605 BC, by their more popular names: Shadrach, Meshach, and Abednego.

As we watch their story unfold in Daniel 3, which is the last time we will see these men in this book, we will see men of courage, conviction, and commitment. These are Psalm 1 men, Psalm 101 men. These are Titus 2 men, 1 Timothy 6:11-21 men. These are men sold out to God in a way that our churches desperately need in our own day. These are men in rare supply. I often say that a good woman is worth her weight in gold, but a good man is worth twice his weight in gold. Why? Not because men are more significant or more important than women, but because of the law of supply and demand. There are too few good men. There are too few who are willing to take a stand for the God who loves them and has saved them.

It is popular to talk of those who show what we call courage under fire. In this passage we will see three men who demonstrate courage *in* the fire! Their faith is amazing. Their confidence in God is stellar. Missionary George Verwer says, "We who have Christ's eternal life need to throw away our own lives" (Newell, *Expect Great Things*, 50). These men were willing to do just that, and as a result we have one of the most famous and remarkable stories in the whole Bible.

God's People Will Be Confronted with the Idols of This World

DANIEL 3:1-7

Although we have no way of knowing how much time has elapsed between them, Daniel 3 follows closely on the heels of Daniel 2. The Septuagint, the Greek translation of the Old Testament, says Daniel 3 took place in the eighteenth year of Nebuchadnezzar's reign (587–586 BC). This is the time when he destroyed the temple in Jerusalem and deported, for a third time, Jews to Babylon. This is reasonable but not certain. Daniel had interpreted Nebuchadnezzar's dream of a great statue (2:31-45), telling him that as the head of gold (2:38) he would have an awesome and powerful kingdom. But he was only the head and not the whole statue. His would be a kingdom that would not endure.

Nebuchadnezzar paid homage and praise to Daniel's God (2:46-47), but it was a shallow and surface praise that would not last long. In fact, 3:1-7 suggests that Nebuchadnezzar did not accept God's will that he was only the head of gold and a temporary king. He wanted it all; therefore, he set up a great gold statue ninety feet high by nine feet wide, gold plated from head to toe (v. 1). It probably looked like a missile on a launching pad, perhaps something like the Washington Monument. Our text goes to great lengths to note the idolatrous nature of this statue of gold. The word "statue" (Aramaic *tselem*) occurs more than ten times in the chapter. Whether this is an image to a particular god (possibly Marduk or Nabu) or an image to Nebuchadnezzar we cannot say. It probably involved both! Either way Dale Davis is right:

> The story is first commandment material (Exod. 20:2). . . .
> The writer holds before you this episode because he wants you
> to make the same response as Daniel's friends: I will believe
> and obey the first commandment even if it kills me (and it
> may). (*Message of Daniel*, 51)

That the pressure on these Hebrews, now young men, would have been enormous cannot be overstated. Note the following details: *First*, it was "set up" in a unique location on the plain of Dura in the province of Babylon (v. 1). Dura simply means "wall" or "fortress," so we cannot be certain of a specific location (Longman, *Daniel*, 97). The mention of Babylon recalls the story of the tower of Babylon (Gen 11) and its goal of unifying all the nations, all the *ethnes* on the earth.

Second, the Who's Who, the movers and shakers of Nebuchadnezzar's vast empire, were invited to the dedication service (v. 2). *Third*, Nebuchadnezzar set a time when national and religious allegiance to him would be put on public display with everyone participating (v. 3). This was a service of national, political, and religious unification. *Fourth*, grand and emotional music was to accompany the moment of dedication, adding a powerful psychological element to the service (v. 5). *Fifth*, a precise moment is specified for the time of submission and worship (v. 5).

Sixth, there is a death warning to anyone who refuses to "fall down and worship" (v. 6). *Seventh*, when the moment of commitment came, it appeared that everyone present pledged allegiance to Nebuchadnezzar and his idolatrous image (v. 7).

While we may not be confronted in the precise way these Hebrew men were, we can be certain the idols of our day will present themselves to us again and again. Some may come quietly and without drawing much attention. Others, however, will be public and put on display for many to witness. When that happens, what will you do? We may not live in the ancient city of Babylon, but we are exiles in a foreign land that is not our home, and idols can be seductive. The fact is, many idols are good things when properly viewed and used. But when a good thing becomes a god thing, it then becomes a bad thing. It becomes an idol. And do not be in doubt or deceived: God's people will be confronted with the idols of this world.

God's People Will Be Criticized by the People of This World
DANIEL 3:8-12

Honoring and obeying God are not always popular. Sometimes they get us into serious problems and even life-threatening situations. While the latter may not often be the experience of Christians in America, it is a daily reality for many of our brothers and sisters around the world.

Simply trying to live a life that is faithful to the God and Savior they love leads them to be criticized, ostracized, and hated. Still, with the apostle Peter they will declare by words and actions, "We must obey God rather than people" (Acts 5:29).

When the time came to bow down and worship the golden image King Nebuchadnezzar had set up, three men conspicuously remained standing: the three Hebrew men known in Babylon as Shadrach, Meshach, and Abednego (3:12). There was no spectacle or outburst of protest, just a quiet and simple act of civil disobedience. Quickly, however, their enemies sprang into action, as "some Chaldeans" (NIV, "astrologers") came forward (v. 8). Andrew Hill notes, "The accusers are either Babylonian officials generally or members of a special guild of diviners or priestly class of wise men" ("Daniel," 79). I have no doubt that they were rivals to the three Hebrew men and jealous of their significant positions in Nebuchadnezzar's administration. It is possible they were also anti-Semitic (e.g., like Haman in Esth 3:5-6; see also Ps 83:1-5). They stepped forward to "maliciously accuse the Jews." Literally, "They ate their pieces!" They sank their teeth into them!

This approach was a strategic one, for the evil one is a scheming and wise serpent. They butter up the king with a common but reverential word of praise, "May the king live forever" (v. 9). But then they give him a subtle and backhanded word of criticism that would strike at his "mega-pride." They remind him that he gave the command to everyone to bow and worship the idol (v. 10) and decreed that everyone who failed to do so would face immediate execution (v. 11). Then they remind him that "there are some Jews *you have appointed* to manage the province of Babylon" (emphasis added). These are your boys, Nebuchadnezzar, and (1) they "ignored you, the king"; they don't respect you and who you are. (2) "They do not serve your gods" either. (On this one the accusers were correct!) (3) Nor do they "worship the gold statue you have set up."

Interestingly, the idea of the king setting up or establishing his idol appears seven times in this passage. This stands in striking contrast to Daniel 2:21, where Daniel tells Nebuchadnezzar, "[God] changes the times and seasons; he removes kings and establishes kings." Nebuchadnezzar is playing a role that only God plays! And in the process he is setting up a showdown that he is going to lose. But it certainly appears that Shadrach, Meshach, and Abednego are in a no-win situation. The critics have come out in the open; they have carefully called out the king, and now he must do something to save face. The stage is set; and things do not look promising for these three Jewish men, these devoted disciples of "the God of the heavens" (2:18,36,44). He gave them favor and wisdom in chapter 1. The pressing question before us is, Now what will he do?

God's People Will Be Challenged to Worship the Gods of This World

DANIEL 3:13-15

It takes courage not to compromise, and your mind needs to be made up before the pressure comes. If you wait until "the moment of truth," you may find out it is too late.

Nebuchadnezzar set up an image made of gold to glorify himself and unify his kingdom. Everything was moving along nicely until these three Jews (v. 8) refused to go along to get along. To say that the head of the Babylonian government was unimpressed by their religious convictions is an understatement. Nebuchadnezzar was "in furious rage." The three Jews had resisted the herd mentality and bravely stood alone. (Apparently Daniel was not present, for there is no doubt he would have stood with them.) Nebuchadnezzar commanded that they be brought before him (v. 13). He questioned them, asking if the accusations were true that they would not serve his gods or "worship" (used eleven times in this chapter: vv. 5,6,7,10,11,12,14,15[2x],18,28) the golden statue he had set up (v. 14). But before moving to their execution, he gave them a second chance (v. 15). Maybe he suspected they had been accused by jealous rivals. Perhaps he genuinely liked them and was looking to provide a way out of this political mess. If they would simply repent of disobeying the king, bow down, and worship his idol, all would be well and good. But if they did not, they would be immediately put to death by being burned alive in the fiery furnace. The options are clear and plain.

In providing them a second chance, Nebuchadnezzar asked the question that is the key to the entire episode: "Who is the god who can rescue you from *my power*?" (emphasis added). I know we do not naturally incline ourselves to identify with Nebuchadnezzar at this point, but I suspect we should. Do we not sometimes exalt ourselves beyond what we should? Do we not often act as if matters of destiny are in our hands and not God's? Do we not draw attention to who *we* are, whom *we* know, and what *we* have done? Is not the same pride that is in the heart of this king lurking in our own? I want so badly to identify with these three Jewish men, but before I do I must first ask, Who is the God who will deliver me from my sin, pride, and arrogance? Who will deliver me from me?

The three Jews know the answer to the king's question, and they will give it in verse 17. They will not trust in themselves, and they will not trust in the powers of this world even if it costs them everything. They will stand strong and trust in "the Most High God" (see Gen 14:18-20,22). Nebuchadnezzar's question indeed is the question of the ages: "Who is the God who will deliver?" The three Jews were glad he asked. The question had been settled in their hearts long ago. If challenged to worship the gods of this world and be praised or worship the one true and living God and be burned to a crisp, it is no contest. As Joshua said, so would they: "As for me and my family, we will worship the LORD" (Josh 24:15).

On September 27, 2015, the president of the United States of America spoke at a Democratic National Committee LGBT fund-raiser. Speaking on the topic of same-sex marriage, the president stated, "We affirm that we cherish our religious freedom, and we are profoundly respectful of religious traditions." So far so good. However, the president went on to say, "But we also have to say that our religious freedom doesn't grant us the freedom to deny our fellow Americans their constitutional rights" (Jackson, "Obama: Don't Use Religion"). Was the president saying that in the final analysis government trumps God? Should the constitution be obeyed above Christ? Such questions should not surprise us. They were raised in Babylon twenty-five hundred years ago.

God's People Must Be Courageous in the Face of Danger in This World
DANIEL 3:16-18

In his passion to get the gospel to every nation, tribe, people, and language (Rev 5; 7), God sends us to the nations. And sometimes in his wondrous providence he sends the nations to us. The latter is what he did on this fateful day in the lives of his three faithful servants in Babylon. Note the *crowd* in verses 2, 3, 4, 7, and 29. All the nations will hear what these men are about to say. Now note the *confession* of Shadrach, Meshach, and Abednego in verses 16-18 before the most powerful political and governmental official on the earth in that day. These men have embraced a countercultural lifestyle with full and complete confidence in God's power and God's purposes.

Regardless of what the immediate outcome might be, three things were clear. First, God's servants will bow down only to God and no one else. Second, God's servants will trust in God's sovereign purposes no matter what. Third, God's servants will trust in God's power and protection and leave what happens to his providential plan. Though the words of Jesus would not be spoken for another six hundred years, I wonder if the Holy Spirit had already put the concept of Mark 13:9-11 into the hearts of these three men:

> But you, be on your guard! They will hand you over to local courts, and you will be flogged in the synagogues. You will stand before governors and kings because of me, as a witness to them. And it is necessary that the gospel be preached to all nations. So when they arrest you and hand you over, don't worry beforehand what you will say, but say whatever is given to you at that time, for it isn't you speaking, but the Holy Spirit.

Shadrach, Meshach, and Abednego tell Nebuchadnezzar the king, "We don't need to give you an answer to this question" (3:16). For them the facts are clear: they did not bow down and worship. Furthermore, their hearts and minds on this issue were made up a long time ago. And finally, they will not adopt some spineless compromise that says something like this: "Well, we will bow on the outside, but we are really standing in the inside." That is not an option for them!

If things proceed as threatened, "Our God whom we serve is able to deliver us . . . and he will deliver us out of your hand, O king" (v. 17 ESV). They know beyond a shadow of a doubt God's power. However, they do not always know his plans and purposes. And neither do we. So they utter one of the greatest affirmations of faith in the whole Bible: "But even if he does not rescue us, we want you as king to know that we will not serve your gods or worship the gold statue you set up." This is a missionary declaration to the nations of absolute trust in their God and only their God. Deliverance and rescue are not the issues. Confession and obedience are, even if they cost them their lives. Their God and only their God "is worthy of the ultimate sacrifice" (Pierce, *Daniel*, 57). I love the *ESV Study Bible*'s note on verse 18:

> There was no doubt in the three men's mind as to God's power to save them (see 2:20-23). Yet the way in which God would work out his plan for them in this situation was less clear. God's power is sometimes extended in dramatic ways to

deliver his people, as when he parted the Red Sea for Israel on the way out of Egypt (Exodus 14); at other times, that same power is withheld, and his people are allowed to suffer. Either way, they would not bow down to Nebuchadnezzar's image.[2]

Nate Saint (1923–56) was martyred as a missionary to the Huaorani people group, the Auca Indians, in Ecuador. His willingness to die for Christ should not surprise us when we consider these words of his:

> The way I see it, we ought to be willing to die. In the military, we were taught that to obtain our objectives we had to be willing to be expendable. Missionaries must face that same expendability. (Newell, *Expect Great Things,* 51)

I would simply add that every follower of the crucified Nazarene should have that same sense of expendability. Jesus is worth it. And he will give you the courage and strength to do it. After all, our God is able!

God's People Can Be Confident the Lord Is with Them No Matter What Happens in This World
DANIEL 3:19-30

The great missionary to Burma, Adoniram Judson, wrote,

> How great are my obligations to spend and be spent for Christ! What a privilege to be allowed to serve him . . . and suffer for him. . . . But in myself I am absolute nothingness. . . . Soon we shall be in heaven. Oh, let us live as we shall then wish we had done! (Newell, *Expect Great Things,* 51).

How I love this man's heart! I think our Hebrew friends would have loved it too.

Once again the head of state is "filled with rage" (cf. v. 13). "The expression [lit. 'image'] on his face changed" against the three Hebrews, and "he gave orders to heat the furnace seven times more than was customary" (v. 19), meaning, "Heat it as hot as you possibly can."

He ordered "some of the best soldiers in his army," his Army Rangers, to bind the three men and "throw them into the furnace of blazing fire" (v. 20). Most certainly they would have dropped them down through an

---

[2] *The Holy Bible: English Standard Version: The ESV Study Bible,* 1592.

opening at the top of the furnace. Another opening at ground level in front would give the king and his subjects a clear view of what happens to those who put their trust in a puny god and disobey the gods of real power. Remember, Nebuchadnezzar had soundly defeated Israel. Therefore it only seemed reasonable to assume his gods were superior to any god these Hebrews had to offer. Their immediate cremation would certainly leave no doubt!

The three Hebrews "were tied up and thrown into the furnace of blazing fire" fully clothed (v. 21). No doubt this would add fuel for the fire. The furnace was so hot the mighty men from the army were immediately consumed and killed (v. 22). As they perished, their last act of submission and obedience to the megalomaniacal king was to push Shadrach, Meshach, and Abednego "bound, into the furnace of blazing fire" (v. 23). Nebuchadnezzar and his loyal, pagan, idolatrous subjects could now sit back and watch what would certainly be a brief human barbecue, an object lesson for all who pledge their allegiance to a god no one can see instead of to the gods of this world who wield true power.

But then something unexpected happened. The king himself was astonished and "jumped up in alarm" (v. 24). "Didn't we throw three men, bound, into the fire?" he asked his advisers. They responded in the affirmative, at which point the king knew he had a problem. First, the Hebrews did not die. In fact, they were no longer bound and were walking around unhurt as if being in a burning fiery furnace was no big deal (v. 25). Second, and more important, there were now *four* guys walking around in the furnace, and the fourth had the appearance "like a son of the gods." In verse 28 Nebuchadnezzar calls the fourth person an angel. However, I think there is a better answer. Some believe this is a theophany, a manifestation of God's presence. I believe it is this, but more. I believe this is what is called a *Christophany*, a preincarnate appearance of the Second Person of the Trinity, the Son of God. The Lord was in there with them. The God who did not deliver them *from* the fire was the God who met them *in* the fire and delivered them *out of* the fire!

Nebuchadnezzar invited the three Jewish men out of the furnace for all to see "that the fire had no effect" on them (v. 27). In fact "not a hair of their heads was singed, their robes were unaffected, and there was no smell of fire on them." He rightly attributed this to "the God of Shadrach, Meshach, and Abednego" (v. 28), the God he called "the Most High God" (v. 26), the One he earlier had called "God of gods, Lord of kings" (2:47). God "quenched the raging of fire" (Heb 11:34), delivered those who "trusted in him" (Dan 3:28), and saved those who "yielded up their bodies rather than serve and worship any god except their God" (ESV; cf. Rom 12:1-2).

As a result of the miracle in the furnace, the king issued a universal decree that if anyone spoke against this God, they would be summarily executed and their houses destroyed (3:29). Since only the Most High God can deliver from such an end, their fate would be sealed. They would die with no hope of rescue.

In the process of events, the king rewarded the three Hebrews in his kingdom (v. 30). Nebuchadnezzar once again experienced (as in chapter 2) conviction when he met the Most High God. However, conviction is not conversion! Like the beast of Revelation 13, the antichrist, Nebuchadnezzar would still have an image that citizens must worship or die. Like that beast he thought he would have a kingdom that never ends. Like that beast he too was badly mistaken.

Charles Spurgeon said it so well: "Beloved, you must go into the furnace if you would have the nearest and dearest dealings with Christ Jesus" (*Sermons on the Book of Daniel*, 3). These Hebrew men did just that. And they experienced exactly what Spurgeon says will happen when we do. When you walk into a fiery furnace, rest assured, Jesus is already there waiting for you.

Conclusion: How Does Our Text Point to Christ?

When Nebuchadnezzar looked into the fiery furnace, he saw four men, not three. The fourth, he said, "looks like a son of the gods" (v. 25). Later he said he was an angel (v. 28). That is not a bad guess for a pagan polytheist. We, however, know better. We can say with confidence the fourth person in the furnace was the one we know as Immanuel, "God is with us" (Matt 1:23). Some are hesitant to make a specific identification with the heavenly being as a preincarnate appearance of the Son of God. In all honesty I feel no such hesitation. I believe the One who walked with them in and through the fire is also the One who walked through the fires of hell on our behalf, in order that we too would not have a single cell of our souls singed by the fiery flames we actually deserve. This should not surprise us. The promises of an ever-present Savior with his people are a resounding theme throughout the Bible:

> *Then he continued, "I am the God of your father, the God of Abraham, the God of Isaac, and the God of Jacob." Moses hid his face because he*

*was afraid to look at God. . . . "I will certainly be with you, and this
will be the sign to you that I am the one who sent you: when you bring
the people out of Egypt, you will all worship God at this mountain."*
(Exod 3:6,12)

*I will be with you when you pass through the waters, and when you
pass through the rivers, they will not overwhelm you. You will not be
scorched when you walk through the fire, and the flame will not burn
you.* (Isa 43:2)

*All authority has been given to me in heaven and on earth. Go,
therefore, and make disciples of all nations, baptizing them in the
name of the Father and of the Son and of the Holy Spirit, teaching
them to observe everything I have commanded you. And remember, I
am with you always, to the end of the age.* (Matt 28:18-20)

*No, in all these things we are more than conquerors through him who
loved us. For I am persuaded that neither death nor life, nor angels
nor rulers, nor things present nor things to come, nor powers, nor
height nor depth, nor any other created thing will be able to separate us
from the love of God that is in Christ Jesus our Lord.* (Rom 8:37-39)

I will never leave you or abandon you. (Heb 13:5)

*Dear friends, don't be surprised when the fiery ordeal comes among you
to test you as if something unusual were happening to you. Instead,
rejoice as you share in the sufferings of Christ, so that you may also
rejoice with great joy when his glory is revealed. If you are ridiculed for
the name of Christ, you are blessed, because the Spirit of glory and of
God rests on you.* (1 Pet 4:12-14)

I love the way James Montgomery Boice closes his sermon on Daniel
3 entitled "Faith in the Furnace." It brings encouragement, hope, and
joy to my soul; and it is my prayer it will do the same for you as you
demonstrate courage in the fire for the One who has delivered us from
an eternal fire, a fire he endured in our place!

> It is not difficult to know who that fourth person was. He was
> Jesus Christ in a preincarnate form—perhaps the form he
> had when he appeared to Abraham before the destruction
> of Sodom and Gomorrah or in which he wrestled with Jacob
> beside the brook Jabbok. It is a vivid portrayal of the fact that

God stands with his people in their troubles. We sing in one of our hymns:

> When through the deep waters I call thee to go,
> The rivers of woe shall not thee overflow:
> For I will be with thee thy troubles to bless,
> And sanctify to thee thy deepest distress.

> When through fiery trials thy pathways shall lie,
> My grace, all sufficient, shall be thy supply;
> The flame shall not hurt thee; I only design
> Thy dross to consume, and thy gold to refine. (*Daniel,* 47)

Reflect and Discuss

1. What are some situations in which you may have to show courage under fire the way Shadrach, Meshach, and Abednego had to in this text?
2. Nebuchadnezzar's homage to Daniel's God in chapter 2 was shallow and short lived. How can we discern when praise and repentance are genuine?
3. The Hebrew men faced enormous pressure to conform. How does our culture pressure believers to reject God and conform to the status quo?
4. What are some of the idols of our day that vie for our worship?
5. How are you tempted to react when accusers and critics come against you? How does this line up with the reactions of Shadrach, Meshach, and Abednego?
6. Why is it often too late to develop our convictions in the moment of truth?
7. Why must we identify with King Nebuchadnezzar before we try to identify with the three Jews?
8. What does it mean to view your life as expendable for the sake of God's kingdom? What did these three men care about more than their lives?
9. When God doesn't deliver us from dangers, trials, disease, or even death, does that mean he has abandoned us? Why or why not?
10. How does the presence of Christ affect the way you face temptations to worship and chase after other gods?

Learning the Hard Way That God Is God and We Are Not

DANIEL 4:1-37

Main Idea: Because God is supremely glorious, he will not allow others to steal his glory, and he graciously humbles all who proudly trust in themselves.

I.   **It Is Good to Honor Our Great and Sovereign God for Sorrow That Leads to Repentance (4:1-3).**
II. **It Is Good When Our Great and Sovereign God Troubles Our Hearts in Order to Get Our Attention (4:4-18).**
III. **It Is Good When Our Great and Sovereign God Exposes Our Sin and Calls Us to Righteousness (4:19-27).**
IV. **It Is Good That Our Great and Sovereign God Humbles Us When We Are Arrogant and Prideful (4:28-33).**
V.   **It Is Good to Praise Our Great and Sovereign God Because He Always Does What Is Right (4:34-37).**

C. S. Lewis calls it "the great sin" and with good reason. It is the sin that led to the fall of Satan. It is the sin that led to the fall of humanity and drove Adam and Eve from the garden of Eden. Of this sin Lewis said,

> There is one vice of which no man in the world is free; which everyone loathes when he sees it in someone else; and of which hardly any people, except Christians, ever imagine that they are guilty themselves. I have heard people admit that they are bad-tempered, or that they cannot keep their heads about girls or drink, or even that they are cowards. I do not think I have ever heard anyone who was not a Christian accuse himself of this vice. And at the same time I have very seldom met anyone, who was not a Christian, who showed the slightest mercy to it in others. There is no fault that makes a man more unpopular, and no fault which we are more unconscious of in ourselves. And the more we have it ourselves, the more we dislike it in others.

The vice I am talking of is Pride or Self-Conceit: and the virtue opposite to it, in Christian morals, is called Humility. . . . According to Christian teachers, the essential vice, the utmost evil, is Pride. Unchastity, anger, greed, drunkenness, and all that, are mere fleabites in comparison: it was through Pride that the devil became the devil: Pride leads to every other vice: it is the complete anti-God state of mind. (*Mere Christianity,* 121–22)

Jonathan Edwards had much the same opinion on this great sin as Lewis:

The first, and the worst cause of errors that prevail in such a state of things, is spiritual pride. This is the main door, by which the Devil comes into the hearts of those that are zealous for the advancement of religion. 'Tis the chief inlet of smoke from the bottomless pit, to darken the mind, and mislead the judgment: this is the main handle by which the Devil has hold of religious persons, and the chief source of all the mischief that he introduces, to clog and hinder a work of God. This cause of error is the mainspring, or at least the main support of all the rest. Till this disease is cured, medicines are in vain applied to heal other diseases. . . .

Pride is much more difficultly discerned than any other corruption, for that reason that the nature of it does very much consist in a person's having too high a thought of himself: but no wonder that he that has too high a thought of himself don't know it; for he necessarily thinks that the opinion he has of himself is what he has just grounds for, and therefore not too high. . . . The heart is so deceitful and unsearchable in nothing in the world, as it is in this matter, and there is no sin in the world, that men are so confident in, and so difficultly convinced of: the very nature of it is to work self-confidence, and drive away [humility]. (*Some Thoughts on the Revival,* 414–16)

Proverbs 8:13 teaches us, "To fear the LORD is to hate evil. I hate arrogant pride, evil conduct, and perverse speech." Perhaps no one in the Bible came to understand this truth better than King Nebuchadnezzar of Babylon. Proud of his accomplishments and proud in his speech, he learned the hard way that "pride comes before destruction, and an arrogant spirit before a fall" (Prov 16:18). He learned the hard way that you can be strutting like a king one day and living like an animal the next. He learned the hard way that the "Most High" God (Dan 4:2,17,24,25,32,34) is God, and he and we are not.

God hates pride because it challenges his sovereignty and questions his will and ways (4:37). It claims a position and power for mere mortals that rightly belongs only to "the King of the heavens" (v. 37). Daniel 4, through the humiliation and restoration of the most powerful man on the earth in that day, reminds us that God is in control and we are not. He is sovereign over all and "is ruler over human kingdoms" (4:17,25,32). These are words of assurance and comfort. They are also words of warning and wisdom for all of us. What God did to King Nebuchadnezzar, he can also do—and will do if necessary—to you and me. This is the last that we will see of Nebuchadnezzar in Daniel. The text contains a powerful warning concerning the pitfalls of pride. It also contains "a powerful message for those who are fearful of or intimidated by the might of human kings and kingdoms" (Greidanus, *Preaching Christ from Daniel*, 113).

It Is Good to Honor Our Great and Sovereign God for Sorrow That Leads to Repentance
DANIEL 4:1-3

Before his downfall a person's heart is proud, but humility comes before honor.

Proverbs 18:12

Do you wish people to think well of you? Don't speak well of yourself.

Blaise Pascal, *Pensées*, 1670

Chapter 4 begins like chapter 3 ends: with a kingly decree. It is also similar to chapter 2, with the king having a dream and needing an interpretation from Daniel. Once again, his magicians, enchanters, Chaldeans, and astrologers cannot deliver the goods (v. 7). They are as impotent in chapter 4 as they were in chapter 2. However, this decree in chapter 4 is cut from a different cloth. It is a personal testimony, a gospel tract, and a deposition before a judge and jury all wrapped up in one amazing story. In making this decree, Nebuchadnezzar wishes to honor the Most High God for what he did to lead him (or drive him!) to a sorrow that led to repentance.

He begins by noting the universal, even missional, nature of what he is about to share by addressing "every people, nation, and language, who live on the whole earth" (v. 1). If Nebuchadnezzar were alive today, he would have called a prime-time news conference for TV and radio. He would have used Twitter, Instagram, and Facebook. He wanted as many people as possible to know what God did.

In language steeped in biblical terminology—perhaps an indication that Daniel assisted him in composing this global proclamation—the king begins with a blessing: "May your prosperity increase." This does not sound like the Nebuchadnezzar of chapters 1–3, where he threatens to separate heads from bodies and throws teenagers into a fiery furnace. What changed him? Nebuchadnezzar knows what God did, and he wants the whole world to know: "I am pleased to tell you about the miracles and wonders the Most High God has done for me" (v. 2). He wants to tell of the amazing things the amazing God has done in his life.

Verse 3 is likened to a short hymn of praise or a doxology that, along with the doxology in verse 37, brackets the chapter. The words recall Psalm 145:13. Two parallel affirmations make up the doxology: "How great are [God's] miracles, and how mighty his wonders! His kingdom is an eternal kingdom, and his dominion is from generation to generation." No God is like this God in what he does. And no God is like this God in what he has.

Nebuchadnezzar's worldview and spiritual perspective had been turned on their heads. Because of God's work of bringing great sorrow that led to repentance, he was a new man. C. S. Lewis once more provides a really good insight: "A proud man is always looking down on things and people; and, of course, as long as you are looking down, you cannot see something that is above you" (*Mere Christianity,* 124). Nebuchadnezzar had been looking down, but he is now looking up and he glorifies the God he sees.

It Is Good When Our Great and Sovereign God Troubles Our Hearts in Order to Get Our Attention
DANIEL 4:4-18

In his pride the wicked man does not seek [God]; in all his thoughts there is no room for God.

Psalm 10:4 NIV

If you plan to build a tall house of virtues, you must first lay
deep foundations of humility.

Augustine

Nebuchadnezzar begins his story in verse 4 by recounting the second
troubling dream he received from God (the first was in ch. 2). He notes
that life was good, that he "was at ease in [his] house and flourishing in
[his] palace." Though we cannot be certain, it was probably late in his
reign (605–562 BC), maybe between 575 and 563 BC. He was successfully secure and enjoying a well-deserved time of rest and relaxation, as
he saw it. However, God hit him right between the eyes with a personal
crisis through "a dream" that "frightened [him]" (v. 5). In fact, as he
lay in his bed, he said, "The images and visions in my mind alarmed
me." This dream was another nightmare to which the king would have
attached futuristic significance. So, as he had done previously (2:2-3),
he called his pagan wise men to interpret the dream (4:6). And like the
fool who keeps doing the same thing over and over expecting different
results, he finds out that his scholarly guild again cannot deliver: "They
could not make its interpretation known to me" (v. 7). So once more he
goes to where he should have started. He calls on his go-to guy Daniel,
also named Belteshazzar, noting that "a spirit of the holy gods is in him"
(v. 8). He also identifies Daniel as the "head of the magicians" (which
makes one wonder why Nebuchadnezzar did not go to him first), telling
him that "no mystery puzzles you" (v. 9).

Nebuchadnezzar than tells Daniel his dream in verses 10-17, making
a second request for its interpretation in verse 18. Nebuchadnezzar
saw an incredibly large, strong tree that, like the tower of Babylon in
Genesis 11:1-9, reached into the heavens and "was visible to the ends
of the earth" (4:10-11). It also had beautiful leaves and fruit to feed
everybody. Animals found shade under it, the birds lived in its branches,
and everyone "was fed from it" (v. 12). If this tree represents the king,
and it does, what a testimony and witness to his greatness and glory.
However, tragedy is on the way.

In his vision, while dreaming in bed, he saw an angel "coming down
from heaven." The angel is described as "a watcher, a holy one" (v. 13).
Interestingly, the word "watcher" occurs only in Daniel 4 (vv. 13,17,23)
in the Old Testament. His message is ominous:

> Cut down the tree and chop off its branches; strip off its leaves and
> scatter its fruit. Let the animals flee from under it, and the birds from

its branches. But leave the stump with its roots in the ground and with a band of iron and bronze around it in the tender grass of the field. Let him be drenched with dew from the sky and share the plants of the earth with the animals. Let his mind be changed from that of a human, and let him be given the mind of an animal for seven periods of time. (4:14-16)

Verse 17 is the key that unlocks the purpose of the chapter and the interpretation of the dream. The sentence of judgment on the tree is "by decree of the watchers" for the purpose that "the living will know that the Most High is ruler over human kingdoms. He gives it to anyone he wants and sets the lowliest of people over it." As Bryan Chapell reminds us, "Talent, brains, and opportunity mean nothing apart from God's provision" (*Gospel According to Daniel*, 75). I suspect Nebuchadnezzar had a strong inkling as to the meaning of his visions. Still, he pleads with Daniel to provide the interpretation because, affirming what he knows to be true for the third time, "you have a spirit of the holy gods" (v. 18). The king did not need a yes man. He needed a truth man. The head of state needed a man of faith to speak truth into his life, and Daniel was such a man. Would that we might boldly and humbly walk in his steps!

It Is Good When Our Great and Sovereign God Exposes Our Sin and Calls Us to Righteousness
DANIEL 4:19-27

Everyone with a proud heart is detestable to the LORD; be assured, he will not go unpunished.

Proverbs 16:5

Nothing will make us so tender to the faults of others, as, by self-examination, thoroughly to know our own.

François Fénelon, *The Inner Life*, 1697

Daniel, the man of God, is now stunned and alarmed (NIV, "perplexed" and "terrified," v. 19). I do not think he feared for his life; I think he feared for what might happen to Nebuchadnezzar. I think Daniel genuinely cared for the king. They had spent many years together, and he had a genuine affection for him. However, compassion does not get in the way of conviction (and commission) for the man of God. They can and should complement each other. Nebuchadnezzar, interestingly, seeks to comfort Daniel: "Belteshazzar, don't let the dream or its interpretation alarm you" (v. 19). Daniel responds by saying he wished the dream were not about Nebuchadnezzar but about "those who hate you, and its interpretation to your enemies!" However, Daniel must, as Ephesians 4:15 says, speak the truth in love. He does not stutter or stammer but gives it to the king directly. Like Moses before Pharaoh, Elijah before Ahab and the prophets of Baal, John the Baptist before Herod, and Jesus before Pilate, Daniel tells Nebuchadnezzar not what he wants to hear but what he needs to hear. We can summarize Daniel's interpretation in straightforward and simple propositions:

- You, O King, are the great tree, and it symbolizes your greatness (vv. 20-22).
- You are the tree chopped down with only a stump remaining (v. 23).
- You will live like an animal outdoors in the fields until "seven periods of time" pass (vv. 23-25).
- All of this will happen to teach you a valuable lesson: "that the Most High is ruler over human kingdoms, and he gives them to anyone he wants" (v. 25).
- When you come to your spiritual senses, you will get your kingdom back (v. 26).
- God is a gracious and loving God who is quick to forgive and show mercy. So (a) listen to my counsel, (b) stop your sinning and start doing the right thing, and (c) stop your wicked injustices and show mercy to the oppressed (v. 27). If you do, God may be kind and "perhaps there will be an extension of your prosperity."

I appreciate David Helm's insights into Daniel's interpretation:

> We must be willing to share the bad news with people that they are out of sorts with God, even as our heart breaks for them while saying it. We must be willing to tell others that God is not pleased with this pride—the human tendency to push him aside, and think that we are the measure of all things. We must be willing to say why God works against us—so that we might one day know that he rules, and not us. Finally, we must be ready to call for repentance and offer hope.
>
> Daniel did all of that. And then the text stops. We are not told what the king said on that day. In fact, the verses that

follow take the reader into the future, to at least one year
later, and then seven periods of time beyond. Clearly, God
didn't feel any need for us to know how this private witness
was received. He wanted us simply to see that it was given.
. . . Daniel didn't shirk from speaking God's word into the
life of the most powerful man in the world. In doing so, he
has provided us with an example of the backbone needed to
be faithful when our opportunity comes. And come it will,
for God is in the business of revealing himself to prominent,
powerful people. (*Daniel for You,* 78)

It Is Good That Our Great and Sovereign God Humbles Us When We Are Arrogant and Prideful

DANIEL 4:28-33

*The pride of mankind will be brought low, and human loftiness will be
humbled; the LORD alone will be exalted on that day.*

                                                      Isaiah 2:17

Do not desire to be the principal man in the church. Be lowly.
Be humble. The best man in the church is the man who is
willing to be a doormat for all to wipe their boots on, the
brother who does not mind what happened to him at all, so
long as God is glorified.

         Charles H. Spurgeon, "Micah's Message for To-day," 1889

Nebuchadnezzar pays the price for his "I" and "my" perspective in verse
30. "At the end of twelve months" (v. 29), after Daniel interpreted his
dream and called the king to repentance and mercy (v. 27), "all this
happened to King Nebuchadnezzar" (v. 28). The hammer of God's
judgment came down, and it came down with a vengeance. Bob Fyall
notes, "Nebuchadnezzar is like Adam and Eve who when confronted
with another tree, instead of becoming gods, were banished from Eden"
(*Daniel,* 70).

    Nebuchadnezzar had forgotten who is the Most High and who had
given him his great kingdom. He forgot or chose to ignore Daniel's
warning and call to repentance. "As he was walking on the roof of the
royal palace of Babylon" (v. 29; this was not the only palace he had!),
he began to brag and boast about who he was and what he had done:

"Is this not Babylon the Great that *I* have built to be a royal residence by *my* vast power and for *my* majestic glory?" (v. 30; emphasis added). He essentially said, "I did all this, and I deserve all the praise. I am the smartest. I am the strongest. I am the wisest. I am the man!"

Those who have accomplished great things need to remind themselves daily that they have nothing that God in grace has not given them. We are born where he decides. We are the people he made us to be. The things we have, he gave us. "He gives [them] to anyone he wants" (vv. 17,25). Nebuchadnezzar had forgotten this basic, fundamental truth of life; and now he will be reminded the hard way.

While the king was still crowing about his own greatness, "while the words were still in the king's mouth, a voice came from heaven" (v. 31). A divine thunderclap came down from heaven with a message of severe judgment and sentencing. The Most High who rules the kingdoms of men declares:

- The kingdom is taken from you (v. 31).
- You will be driven away from humanity (v. 32).
- You will live with animals, act like an animal, and eat like an animal (v. 32).
- This will last as long as it takes ("seven periods of time," i.e., seven years or symbolic of the perfect time needed to do the trick), "until you acknowledge that the Most High is ruler over human kingdoms, and he gives them to anyone he wants" (v. 32).

Immediately "the message [of the Most High God] against Nebuchadnezzar was fulfilled" (v. 33). He was struck by what was probably a behavioral disorder called boanthropy, where "one imagines oneself a cow or bull and acts accordingly" (Davis, *Message of Daniel*, 59). It is also referred to as lycanthropy, where a person believes he or she is an animal and behaves like an animal. The one who saw himself as superman became subman. The one who thought he was superhuman became subhuman. He lived with animals instead of with men. He ate grass like an ox, not food like a man. He lived and slept in the field, not in the home and bed of a man. He had fingernails and toenails like the claws of a bird and not those of a human. Sinclair Ferguson is spot on when he says,

> The one who refused to honor God's glory loses his own glory.
> Refusing to share what he has with the poor, he becomes

poorer than the poor. He becomes outwardly what his heart has been spiritually and inwardly—bestial. (*Daniel*, 93)

You might hear the words of Galatians 6:7 whispering in your ears: "Don't be deceived: God is not mocked. For whatever a person sows he will also reap."

It Is Good to Praise Our Great and Sovereign God Because He Always Does What Is Right
DANIEL 4:34-37

God resists the proud, but gives grace to the humble. . . . Humble yourselves before the Lord, and he will exalt you.

James 4:6,10

Jesus came into the world to convert people from God-like dependence on self to child-like dependence on God. And then he died to pay the penalty for our pride and to show us the way to humility and to send all our boasting toward God and not toward ourselves.

John Piper, "Believing God on Election Day," 1988

Psalm 121:1-2 says, "I lift my eyes toward the mountains. Where will my help come from? My help comes from the LORD, the Maker of heaven and earth." I do not know if Nebuchadnezzar knew these verses. What I do know is he not only looked up to the hills, but he also lifted his eyes up to heaven (4:34). After looking down to the ground like an animal, he turned and looked up to God in heaven and was restored to being a man made in the image of the God he had come to know as Savior. Yes, I believe Nebuchadnezzar was genuinely converted and saved and that he entered into a life-changing relationship with the one true and living God, the One he now acknowledged personally as "the Most High." The king's reason returned to him, and he immediately did what any right-thinking person does: he worshiped the only living and true God. He "praised the Most High and honored and glorified him who lives forever," whose dominion is everlasting and whose kingdom goes on forever (vv. 34-35).

In the midst of this song of praise, Nebuchadnezzar gets theological in verse 35. In comparison to the sovereign God whose dominion is everlasting and whose kingdom endures forever, humans are not much:

"All the inhabitants of the earth are counted as nothing." The Most High God does what he wills in heaven above, and he does the same on earth below. You cannot stop this God, and you should not question this God. (I hear Job saying, "Amen!")

Nebuchadnezzar got back his mind, and he also got back his kingdom (v. 36). In fact, God not only set him back on the throne, but "even more greatness came." But this time Nebuchadnezzar did not claim credit for the increase of his kingdom: "Now I, Nebuchadnezzar, praise, exalt, and glorify the King of the heavens." This is the only time the phrase "King of the heavens" appears in the Old Testament. And why does this king on earth praise and extol and honor the King who is in heaven? Three reasons are given: (1) "all his works are true"; (2) "his ways are just"; and (3) "He is able to humble those who walk in pride" (v. 37). These are Nebuchadnezzar's last words in Scripture. He is now dead. He is long gone. However, the King of the heavens, the Most High God, is still on his throne, and he is still sovereign over the universe.

Conclusion: How Does Our Text Point to Christ?

Daniel 4 gives us glimpses of the Lord Jesus in several ways. First, it reminds us to remember who is God and who is not, who is King and who is not. Nebuchadnezzar, as great as he was, was only a finite and temporal king with a small k However, One is coming whom the Ancient of Days will give a dominion and kingdom that will be "an everlasting dominion that will not pass away, and . . . will not be destroyed." In this kingdom "those of every people, nation, and language should serve him" (Dan 7:13-14). This is God's King with a capital K! This is God's Lord with a capital L. This is the King who will rule the nations because he has written "on his robe and on his thigh: KING OF KINGS AND LORD OF LORDS" (Rev 19:16).

Second, we see Christ in striking contrast with Nebuchadnezzar. As Tremper Longman says, "How could those of us who read the New Testament fail to think of Christ in the light of Nebuchadnezzar's pride and shame?" (*Daniel*, 125). Consider the following contrast between the Christ we see in Philippians 2:6-11 and the depiction of Nebuchadnezzar we see in Daniel:

Nebuchadnezzar	Christ
A mere man	Eternal God
Sinful	Sinless
Merciless	Merciful
Glorified himself	Humbled himself
Aspired to sovereignty	Aspired to servanthood
Exalted himself and was humbled by God	Humbled himself and was exalted by God

Third, God gives kingdoms "to anyone he wants and sets the lowliest of people over [them]" (4:17). An ancient Hebrew person reading this verse could easily have thought, *God did this in our past. Will he do it again in our future?* Is there a prophetic impulse in verse 17? Sidney Greidanus notes,

> In Israel's history God set over his kingdom the young David, bypassing his older brothers; he chose the younger Solomon over Adonijah. Isaiah prophesied about God's chosen Servant, "He was despised and rejected by others" (53:3), but God allotted him "a portion with the great" (53:12). . . . Jesus born in a stable, poor, despised, crucified, but claiming after his resurrection that God had given to him "all authority in heaven and on earth" (Matt. 28:18). (*Preaching Christ from Daniel,* 128)

Yes, God had done it before. And yes, God would do it again!

Reflect and Discuss

1. How is pride connected to all other sin?
2. Why is it not arrogant of God to humble everyone whose pride threatens his glory?
3. What indications do we have in this text that Nebuchadnezzar's worship is genuine?
4. Describe a time when God has troubled your heart to get your attention. How did you respond?
5. Why is speaking the truth in love often so hard? How does Daniel model this act of grace?
6. How does Nebuchadnezzar resemble Adam and Eve? How is God's response to the king similar to his response to our first parents?

7. How can someone who experiences great success in this world, like Nebuchadnezzar, remain humble?
8. What is God showing Nebuchadnezzar in making him animal-like?
9. How could Nebuchadnezzar have used his kingdom to honor God instead of trying to steal glory from God? How can you use your gifts, talents, and successes to serve God?
10. How does Jesus model how to handle greatness? How has he used his power to serve others?

The Handwriting Is on the Wall

DANIEL 5:1-31

Main Idea: God sees our sin and rebellion and brings about judgment on those who refuse to repent and trust in him.

I.   God Sees Our Sin When We Mock His Glory (5:1-4).
II. God Confronts Our Sins, and We Should Tremble When He Does (5:5-9).
III. God Exposes Our Sins, and We Are Found Wanting (5:10-28).
IV. God Deals with Our Sins of Unrepentance with Appropriate Judgment (5:29-31).

Two of my favorite movies of all time are *The Godfather* (1972) and *The Godfather: Part II* (1974). They are both classics. In *The Godfather: Part II* there is a scene in which the godfather, Michael Corleone (played by Al Pacino), is in Cuba sealing a deal with the Cuban government that will result in massive wealth for his family. Michael learns of rebel activity that causes some concern, but he is told not to worry because the Cuban government has everything under control. Later, at a grand New Year's celebration put on by President Batista of Cuba, the military leadership marches in to inform the most powerful man in Cuba that his government has collapsed, the rebels will soon have control, and everyone needs to get out immediately and flee to safety. The godfather escapes, and the Cuban government falls into the hands of communist rebels. Pride, arrogance, and a sense of indestructability led them to ignore the handwriting on the wall!

In Daniel 5 there is a literal instance of predictive handwriting on the wall, and this one could not be ignored because what appeared (v. 5) was written by the hand of God. Furthermore, the message God wrote would soon become clear and its promise certain. Anytime and any way God speaks, we should all listen carefully.

In the flow of the book of Daniel, chapter 5 comes out of nowhere, though there is a clear theological connection to the last verse of chapter 4, where we are told that when it comes to the "King of the heavens, . . . all his works are true and his ways are just. He is able to humble those who walk in pride" (4:37). We have been dealing with King Nebuchadnezzar in chapters 1–4, and suddenly we meet King Belshazzar in 5:1. Dale Davis sets the stage for the drama that is about to unfold:

> Nebuchadnezzar died in 562 BC, after a reign of forty-three years. In less than another twenty-five years all was lost. Evil-Merodach (561–560), Nebuchadnezzar's son, followed his father on the throne. He, however, was apparently assassinated by his brother-in-law Neriglissar, who had a tenure of about four years and was succeeded by his son, Labashi-Marduk. This poor creature was "liquidated" within a month and one of the conspirators, Nabonidus, became king (555–539 BC). It seems that Nabonidus did not have designs on the throne himself but may have been placed there as a "compromise candidate" by the conspirators. Some think that Belshazzar, Nabonidus' son, was the real mover behind the conspirators. In any case, Nabonidus had a religious or "faith" problem. He was a passionate devotee of the moon god Sin, to such a degree that he alarmed the Babylonian clergy, for he seemed intent on prying Marduk loose from his supremacy in Babylon. This may have led to a "relocation programme" for Nabonidus—he spent the next ten years at Taima/Tema, an oasis in the North Arabian Desert, five hundred miles from Babylon. His son, Belshazzar, functioned as *de facto* king in Babylon, operated in a more pro-Mardukian manner, and thus kept the local clergy from revolt. Which is why we are suddenly staring Belshazzar (553–539 BC) in the face at Daniel 5. (*The Message of Daniel*, 70–71)

So there is a chronological gap between chapters 4 and 5 of approximately twenty years. We must keep in mind, however, that Daniel was never written to give us a history lesson about Babylonians, Medes, and Persians. It was written to encourage the Hebrew people, God's people, that though they had been defeated and exiled (three times!), God was sovereignly in control and they should trust him even when they could not trace his hand. He is working out his plans and accomplishing his purposes, and every now and then he lets us in on what he is doing. Daniel 5 is another occasion in which God lets us see what he is up to. Like the fiery furnace of chapter 3 and the lion's den of chapter 6, this is one of the most remarkable and memorable stories in the whole Bible. We will see again the truth of Daniel 4:25, "that the Most High is ruler over human kingdoms, and he gives them to anyone he wants" (cf. 5:21). Yes, our God gives kingdoms to whom he wills, and he also takes them away from whom he wills. Belshazzar is about to find that out this very night—on what Ken Gangel calls "the night of bad calls" (*Daniel,* 128). The handwriting on the wall is on the way.

God Sees Our Sin When We Mock His Glory
DANIEL 5:1-4

The last Babylonian king, a man named Belshazzar, decided to throw a big party even as Darius the Mede (5:31; probably another name for Cyrus or even a dynastic title) is about to invade Babylon and bring its empire to a speedy end. To call this event a party is kind. The word "orgy" is probably more appropriate. And it was quite the event, which adds to the irony and foolishness of the moment! This feast was "for a thousand of his nobles." Furthermore, he did something kings normally did not do: he "drank wine in their presence" (v. 1). He set the example of drunkenness, sensuality, and revelry on this fateful night. He would be the life of the party, even as his own life would soon come to an abrupt end. What a fool Belshazzar was!

However, his foolishness did not stop here. He decided to add blasphemy, mockery, idolatry, and sexual immorality to the list. While he was drinking and getting drunk, he "gave orders to bring in the gold and silver vessels that his predecessor Nebuchadnezzar had taken from the temple in Jerusalem" so that his fellow party animals might drink from them. Verse 2 records the command; and verse 3, in almost identical language used to emphasize the blasphemy and mockery of the command, records the response. Belshazzar, along with his lords, numerous wives, and concubines, drank their wine from the sacred vessels taken from Yahweh's temple. Not interested in stopping here, they added idolatrous worship to their debased behavior as they "praised their gods made of gold and silver, bronze, iron, wood, and stone" (v. 4). This almost sounds like an Olympic celebration, considering all the gold, silver, and bronze, but there is nothing noble about this night of debauchery and mockery.

The spiritual and theological significance of all of this cannot be overstated. The act is intended to mock the God of Judah and to celebrate the gods of Babylon as being superior. Appearing in public and drinking with his guests was not traditional protocol for a Babylonian king. No doubt Belshazzar wanted to make this banquet special, and one way to do that was to make a spectacle of Judah's God. Belshazzar takes holy vessels and treats them as nothing more than common utensils. He then goes further and uses them in the worship of false gods. His royal guests, his many wives, and his concubines (his human sex toys) all joined in the frivolity and raunchiness of the evening. Perhaps Belshazzar was attempting to win the favor and protection of his false gods with the enemy at his doorstep. In trusting in those gods who are no gods, he is making the biggest mistake of his life. The wisdom of Proverbs 6:12-15 is about to unfold:

> A worthless person, a wicked man goes around speaking dishonestly, winking his eyes, signaling with his feet, and gesturing with his fingers. He always plots evil with perversity in his heart; he stirs up trouble. Therefore calamity will strike him suddenly; he will be shattered instantly, beyond recovery.

Indeed, the prophecy of Isaiah 47, given more than a hundred years earlier concerning the downfall of Babylon, is about to come to fruition. It is worth taking notice of Isaiah 47:10-11 specifically. There God's Word says,

> You were secure in your wickedness; you said, "No one sees me." Your wisdom and knowledge led you astray. You said to yourself, "I am, and there is no one else." But disaster will happen to you; you will not know how to avert it. And it will fall on you, but you will be unable to ward it off. Devastation will happen to you suddenly and unexpectedly.

Bryan Chappell is right: "There is no human wall so high, no human accomplishment so great, that it is secure against the judgment of God" (*The Gospel According to Daniel*, 97). Belshazzar is about to learn how true this is. Indeed, we all should learn how true this is before it is too late. After all, there is a Belshazzar lurking in all of our hearts. We all need God to deliver us from us!

God Confronts Our Sins, and We Should Tremble When He Does
DANIEL 5:5-9

The Babylonians are having a gala to remember; they are completely out of touch with reality. Sin does this. It makes us dull. It makes us stupid. Sinclair Ferguson is right:

> Belshazzar is perhaps the supreme Old Testament parallel to the rich fool in Jesus' parable. Having already given expression to their lust for more (in the case of the rich fool his lust for more money), they would never be satisfied without more. Blinded by the pursuit of that lust, they were oblivious to the possibility that "This night your soul will be required of you; then whose will those things be which you have provided?" (Luke 12:20). (*Daniel*, 102)

In a moment (ESV, "immediately"), the king is brought to his senses. I'm sure Belshazzar set the record for the shortest time it has ever taken for a drunk to sober up! Ligon Duncan says,

> From verses 5-7 this man goes from a break with reality to a check with reality. Suddenly, Belshazzar is yanked into the reality of the seriousness of the moment. ("The Handwriting on the Wall")

And what yanked him back into reality? "The fingers of a man's hand appeared and began writing on the plaster of the king's palace wall next to the lampstand" (v. 5). Yes, I think that would probably do it! The same fingers that wrote the Ten Commandments for the Hebrew people (Exod 31:18; Deut 9:10) now confront blasphemous Belshazzar with his sins and imminent judgment. Verse 6 records his terrified fourfold response: (1) His facial color changed. A red face flushed from drinking quickly turned as white as a sheet. (2) His mind went into a tizzy. (3) He went slack. (4) His knees knocked together. Dale Davis provides a descriptive and colorful commentary on what might be happening to this shaking sovereign:

> Belshazzar's demeaning of Yahweh's vessels was his way of demeaning Yahweh. Belshazzar was not simply a drunken

> slob but a profane slob. God brought him to almost instant
> sobriety, however. Belshazzar came unglued—he was seeing
> the fingers of a man's hand writing on the palace wall. He
> became deathly pale, his thoughts terrified him, and his lower
> body lost all strength. The clear sight and sheer spookiness
> of those writing fingers produced paralyzing terror (5–6). . . .
> Some think that "his limbs gave way" (v. 6 ESV; lit., "the knots
> of his loins were loosed") may refer to his losing control of
> bladder or bowels. (*The Message of Daniel,* 74)

I think we can all admit that if this was his reaction, it would be hard to
blame him!

The king tries to regain his composure, but it is a bumbling, stumbling
effort to say the least. He "shouted to bring in the mediums, Chaldeans
[NIV, "astrologers"], and diviners." He promised "these wise men of
Babylon" (ha!) honor ("clothed in purple"), wealth ("a gold chain"),
and status ("third highest position in the kingdom," after his father
Nabonidus and himself) if they could read the writing on the wall and
provide the interpretation (v. 7). The foolishness of this move only adds
to the foolishness in verses 1-4. This brain trust, these cardinals of counsel, these intellectual elitists, these PhDs who commanded the respect
of the common man proved once more to be totally useless! These sup-
posedly "wise men of Babylon" could not interpret Nebuchadnezzar's
dream in chapter 2 and had to be bailed out by Daniel. The same thing
happened again in chapter 4! Now, for a third time, "all the king's wise
men" are brought in and once more strike out (v. 8).

Belshazzar's response by now is laughably predictable (v. 9): "Then
King Belshazzar became even more terrified, his face turned pale
[again!], and his nobles were bewildered [NIV, "baffled"]." *The Message*
reads, "So now the king was really frightened. All the blood drained from
his face. The nobles were in a panic." Belshazzar has been confronted
with his sin by a holy and omnipotent God, and he rightly trembles. The
practical and theological insights of Dale Davis are once more helpful as
we contemplate the impact these verses should make on us:

> Where does one turn in such moments? Why, to religion, of
> course. Or at least that's what Belshazzar did. He turned to
> his "faith." He hollered for the conjurers, the Chaldeans, and
> the astrologers (7) to come in and interpret the mysterious
> text. So these losers came traipsing in again (cf. 2:2,10–11,27;

4:7). Once more they fail (8), and Belshazzar's alarm only intensifies (9). This is sometimes God's pattern—to aggravate our helplessness by exposing the uselessness of our favourite props, even our favourite religious props. You may have your own paganism of choice—occultism, pluralism, machoism, feminism, agnosticism, moralism—and they will prove as petrifyingly useless as the Babylonian variety.

The human defiance is quite clear, but you may wonder where the divine opportunity appears. Precisely here, at the end of verse 9! God has frightened Belshazzar; religion has failed him; he is reduced to a shivering, sniffling mess with no supports whatever. He is therefore on the edge of the abyss of hope, is he not? He is the object of God's terror, but in one sense it is a kind terror. God does Belshazzar the favour of leaving him without any recourse, in utter helplessness—and hence with a huge opportunity. Whenever God brings a man to the end of himself, smashing all his props and wasting his idols, it is a favourable moment indeed. If he will but see it. (*Message of Daniel*, 74–75)

God Exposes Our Sins, and We Are Found Wanting
DANIEL 5:10-28

We have arrived at the crisis moment, the moment of truth. David Dorsey calls verses 10-12 the "turning point," and sees them as the apex of a chiastically arranged chapter 5.

Story 5: Belshazzar's feast (5:1-31 [5:1–6:1])
a) Introduction: Belshazzar in prosperity; his feast and
  mockery of Yahweh's vessels (5:1-4)
  b) Handwriting on the wall (5:5-6)
    c) Magicians are summoned; failure of magicians to
      interpret the writing (5:7-9)
      d) TURNING POINT: Daniel is remembered (5:10-12)
    c´) Daniel is summoned; failure of magicians
      recounted (5:13-16)
  b´) Handwriting on the wall interpreted by Daniel (5:17-28)
a´) Conclusion: Daniel is honored, and Belshazzar's kingdom
  is overthrown (5:29-31 [5:29–6:1])

Dorsey notes, "Structured repetition is used throughout Daniel to emphasize the book's two main themes: Yahweh's supremacy over all earthly powers and the importance for Jews to remain loyal to their God even in exile." These two themes are emphasized again, Dorsey says, "by the matching stories about Yahweh's supremacy over the two powerful and proud Babylonian monarchs: Nebuchadnezzar and Belshazzar (chaps. 4, 5)" (*Literary Structure of the Old Testament*, 261–62).

Hearing the loud cry of the king and his lords, the queen, probably Belshazzar's mother, "came to the banquet hall" (5:10). She respectfully addresses the king in a traditional manner ("May the king live forever") and tells him to get a grip on himself because

> *there is a man in your kingdom who has a spirit of the holy gods in him. In the days of your predecessor he was found to have insight, intelligence, and wisdom like the wisdom of the gods. Your predecessor, King Nebuchadnezzar, appointed him chief of the magicians, mediums, Chaldeans, and diviners. . . . [He] did this because Daniel, the one the king named Belteshazzar, was found to have an extraordinary spirit, knowledge and intelligence, and the ability to interpret dreams, explain riddles, and solve problems. (5:11-12)*

Therefore she advises that Daniel be called out of obscurity and retirement "and he will give the interpretation."

Daniel, the man of God, is brought before the king. There may be a subtle insult directed at the old man, now likely in his eighties, as he is referred to as "one of the Judean exiles" (v. 13). Interestingly, the king calls him by his Jewish name. Still, Belshazzar repeats the queen mother's praise of Daniel, revealing that his reputation precedes him (v. 14). The king recounts the failure of his impotent soothsayers (v. 15) and reaffirms his promise of purple, gold, and promotion to third ruler in the kingdom if Daniel can interpret the handwriting on the wall (v. 16).

Daniel's response is not disrespectful, but it is direct. The king can keep his gifts or give them to someone else; Daniel neither needs nor wants them. Yet he "will read the inscription for the king and make the interpretation known to him" (v. 17). (As an aside, that is a pretty good summary of faithful, biblical exposition!) But before Daniel interprets the handwriting, he does a little preaching and schools Belshazzar in recent history and biblical theology. Note that God is referenced five times in verses 18-28. He is called "the Most High God" (vv. 18,21), "the Lord of the heavens" (v. 23), and "the God who holds your life-breath in his hand" (v. 23). Here is a summary of his message in outline form:

- The Most High God gave your predecessor Nebuchadnezzar his kingdom with the glory and privileges that go with such a position (5:18-19).
- Your father became arrogant and prideful, so God took him down and caused him to live like a beast with animals like oxen and donkeys. God did this so he would know that "the Most High God is ruler over human kingdoms and sets anyone he wants over them" (vv. 20-21).
- You, Belshazzar, are just like him, and you should know better! You are even more responsible than your predecessor! You have blasphemed and mocked God with your revelry and idolatry. Indeed, "you have not glorified the God who holds your life-breath in his hand and who controls the whole course of your life" (vv. 22-23).
- Therefore, the Most High God has exposed your sin, weighed your evil and wicked actions, and you are found wanting (vv. 24-28).

Verses 24-28 need further attention if we are to understand what had been written on the wall. The writing on the wall was inscribed in Aramaic as "MENE, MENE, TEKEL, and PARSIN" (5:26). There would have been no vowel markings, and the letters would have run consecutively. Daniel's first step is to rightly separate the letters into the appropriate word divisions. This yields four words to the inscription that reads, "numbered, numbered, weighed, divided." Daniel then provides the devastating interpretation in verses 26-28:

> God has numbered the days of your kingdom and brought it to an end.
> . . . You have been weighed on the balance and found deficient. . . .
> Your kingdom has been divided and given to the Medes and Persians.

God is closing the books on Belshazzar's kingdom. God's measuring standard proves the king to be a lightweight, a loser. He challenged the Most High God and lost. He crossed the line, and the gig is up. God saw his sin just as he sees everyone's sin, and the time of reckoning has come, as it will for all who refuse to bow and humbly submit to "the Most High God." Remember, a day is coming when *every knee will bow—in heaven and on earth and under the earth— and every tongue will confess that Jesus Christ is Lord, to the glory of God the Father.* (Phil 2:10-11)

God Deals with Our Sins of Unrepentance with Appropriate Judgment
DANIEL 5:29-31

Turn out the lights, the party's over. Tell the band they can all go home, and they don't need to come back. Ever! "The Most High God" is taking Belshazzar out and setting up a new world monarch named Cyrus, here identified as Darius the Mede (5:30-31).

Dale Davis points out that "chapters 2, 3, and 4 all end with some 'confession' by Nebuchadnezzar (2:46-47; 3:28-29; 4:34-37), but there is none of that at the end of chapter 5" (*Message of Daniel*, 71). Belshazzar showed no signs of repentance for his arrogance, blasphemies, idolatry, pride, and sensualities. He did however, and probably reluctantly, keep his word to Daniel. Like wicked King Herod who murdered John the Baptist, he no doubt was "exceedingly sorry" because of his oath (Mark 6:26 ESV). But to save face, he had to keep his word. How often our words come back to bite us!

"Belshazzar gave an order," and Daniel was clothed in purple, got his gold chain, and was raised up to "be the third ruler in the kingdom" (5:29). Once again God has honored his faithful servant in this hostile and pagan world. Daniel had been sent to the retirement home by men of power. God brought him out of retirement and made him "third ruler in the kingdom." After Nabonidus and his son Belshazzar, no one was more powerful than the Judean exile (cf. v. 13).

Daniel's ascendancy in the Babylonian Empire was short-lived. It was like getting a promotion the day before the company goes bankrupt. It was like getting a medal on the day your side lost the war. His title lasted only a night. However, Darius will wisely recognize the value of this man of God in the days that follow (cf. 6:3). "That very night Belshazzar the king of the Chaldeans was killed" (5:30)—not exactly the way he expected his party to end.

According to the Greek historians Herodotus (fifth century BC) and Xenophon (ca. 434–355 BC), the Medo-Persian army did not attempt to storm the impregnable Babylonian walls, which were at least forty feet high and twenty-five feet in width. It has to be noted that Herodotus exclaimed, "Babylon surpasses in wonder any city in the known world," and he said the walls were fifty-six miles long, eighty feet thick, and three hundred twenty feet high! While this may have been an exaggeration (thirty stories high!?), no one denies their magnificence. So how did the Medo-Persians get into the city?

> They diverted water from the Euphrates River (which ran under the walls of Babylon) into a marsh. With the level of the water lowered, the soldiers were able to wade the river under the walls and enter the city. Xenophon added that the city was invaded while the Babylonians were feasting in a time of drunken revelry. . . . As a matter of fact, Xenophon cited the festival as the reason the Persians chose to attack Babylon on that particular night. (Miller, *Daniel*, 167)

The dates were October 11–12, 539 BC (ibid.).

Belshazzar bites the dust "and Darius the Mede received the kingdom [from God!] at the age of sixty-two" (v. 31). The Babylonian king had challenged and mocked the Most High God, and it was no contest. He had been confronted with his sin and showed no repentance. So God took him out. On this occasion God's judgment did not come gradually, like a frog being boiled in a kettle. It struck like a lightning bolt from heaven.

To those who knew their Scriptures, this was no surprise. God's prophets had already laid out Babylon's destiny—this kingdom was a passing fad, here today and gone tomorrow (see Isa 21:1-10; Jer 50–51). Sinclair Ferguson directs us to the wisdom of Proverbs (*Daniel*, 114):

> *One who becomes stiff-necked, after many reprimands will be shattered instantly—beyond recovery.* (Prov 29:1)

> *How long, inexperienced ones, will you love ignorance? How long will you mockers enjoy mocking and you fools hate knowledge? If you respond to my warning, then I will pour out my spirit on you and teach you my words. Since I called out and you refused, extended my hand and no one paid attention, since you neglected all my counsel and did not accept my correction, I, in turn, will laugh at your calamity. I will mock when terror strikes you.* (Prov 1:22-26)

In Revelation 18 we read of the destruction of Babylon, that evil and wicked world system that stands against the kingdom of God economically, morally, politically, and spiritually. In Daniel 5, we have received a preview of that eschatological day. Here we find words of wisdom, words of warning.

Conclusion: Where Is Christ in This Text?

In the story of God's handwriting on the wall, a Hebrew exile comes out of nowhere to confront the powers of this world with their sins of blasphemy, mockery, arrogance, pride, and idolatry. Given that Daniel has been off the historical scene for many years, it is almost as if he has risen from the dead. He is a man of impeccable character who cannot be bought or seduced by the idols of this world. Why? Because in this man of unsurpassed wisdom is the Spirit of the Holy God. In fact, even the pagans acknowledge his good testimony (5:11; cf. 3 John 11-12), acknowledging he has "an extraordinary spirit, knowledge and intelligence, and the ability to interpret dreams, explain riddles, and solve problems" (5:12; cf. 6:3).

This sounds rather familiar with respect to another exile from Judah, one who comes on the scene in the first century, a man by the name of Jesus who said of himself, "The Spirit of the Lord is on me, because he has anointed me" (Luke 4:18). Later we are not surprised to hear even his enemies admit, "No man ever spoke like this!" (John 7:46). That Daniel typifies in our text the coming Messiah is hard to deny. This servant of the Lord foreshadows the Servant of the Lord on whom rests

> the Spirit of the Lord . . . a Spirit of wisdom and understanding, a Spirit of counsel and strength, a Spirit of knowledge and of the fear of the Lord. (Isa 11:2)

Daniel's wisdom and abilities and position are similar in many ways to those of the patriarch Joseph (Gen 37–50), and thus his life reflects backward. However, as the mediator of God's wisdom to sinful humanity, his life looks forward to the ultimate mediator between God and humanity, the Lord Jesus Christ (1 Tim 2:5), the one Paul calls "the wisdom of God" in 1 Corinthians 1:24, the one in whom "are hidden all the treasures of wisdom and knowledge" (Col 2:3).

Reflect and Discuss

1. Why do you think we are prone to view ourselves as indestructible or untouchable? How can you see this tendency in your own life?

2. How do Belshazzar's actions serve to mock God and his glory? What are some other ways we implicitly mock God's glory?

3. What are some ways we often try to protect ourselves against God's judgment? How do we try to convince ourselves we are beyond his reach?

4. How and why does sin make us foolish?

5. What kinds of things does God use to wake us up to the foolishness of our sin? How does it feel when he does this?

6. How are God's acts of discipline also acts of grace?

7. How does Daniel model faithful biblical exposition in his interpretation of the dream?

8. How does Belshazzar continue the sins of his predecessor, Nebuchadnezzar?

9. How does Belshazzar's response to God differ from Nebuchadnezzar's?

10. How does Daniel foreshadow Jesus in this passage? In what ways does Jesus more perfectly mediate between God and man than Daniel does?

Daniel and the Lions' Den

DANIEL 6:1-28

Main Idea: Though following God faithfully may be costly, he is Lord over all and is able to deliver his people. His final victory is accomplished in Jesus.

I. **Honor God and Let Him Exalt You (6:1-4).**
   A. Walk in the Spirit (6:1-3).
   B. Serve faithfully (6:4).
II. **Be True to God Even When It May Cost You (6:5-15).**
   A. Evil men will try to entrap a godly man (6:5-9).
   B. Godly men will remain faithful to God no matter what (6:10-15).
III. **Trust that God Is Able to Deliver You (6:16-24).**
   A. We can rest in God's plan (6:16-18).
   B. We can be certain of God's power (6:19-24).
IV. **Recognize God Will Use You to Make His Name Famous among the Nations (6:25-28).**
   A. God can cause unbelievers to acknowledge his greatness (6:25-26).
   B. God can even use unbelievers to proclaim his glory (6:26-28).

Of all the exciting stories in the book of Daniel, none is more famous than the one found in chapter 6. It provokes our imagination. It causes our hearts to skip a beat. We immediately sense similarities with the story of Shadrach, Meshach, and Abednego and the fiery furnace of chapter 3. And the thought of a faithful eighty-year-old man being thrown into a pit with ravenous lions simply for praying grabs us in an almost inexplicable manner. It seems completely unfair because it is.

It is disappointing, but not surprising, to find liberal scholars questioning the authenticity and historicity of the story. Some call it a folk tale or fable, a made-up, make-believe story.[3] They, of course, did the same thing with the fiery furnace story. They attacked, pointing out that Darius

---

[3] For example, see Hartman and Di Lella, *The Book of Daniel*, 196.

the Mede is never mentioned outside the Bible, and suggesting that the author of Daniel, someone writing much later, got confused and used Darius the Persian (521–486 BC; see Neh 12:22) in this fictitious narrative. However, it is possible that Darius functioned as a title and not a proper name. Darius the Mede may be referring to a man named Gubaru, who served as governor of Babylon under Cyrus the Great. Or it could be, as I think, another designation for Cyrus himself, king over the Medo-Persian Empire. If this is so, we would understand Daniel 6:28 to say, "So this Daniel prospered during the reign of Darius, that is, the reign of Cyrus the Persian"—a perfectly legitimate interpretation. Sinclair Ferguson provides a helpful perspective on all of this when he writes,

> It is a sad reflection on the biblical scholarship of the last century that in matters such as these the Bible has been treated as guilty until proved innocent. This attitude stands in marked contrast to the credibility given to other nonbiblical texts of the same period. We need constantly to remind ourselves that no one comes to Scripture with a mind free from a faith commitment; one will either have faith in Scripture as God's Word or one's attitude will be one of unbelief, rejecting Scripture's testimony to its own reliability. God's Word, like God's kingdom, will remain when all the theories that propose its inaccuracy have crumbled into dust. One is reminded of how a nineteenth-century book that attacked the reliability of Scripture was later pulped and the recycled paper used to print Bibles. (*Daniel*, 116–17)

We gladly and confidently, therefore, approach this passage as a real story about a real man who by supernatural protection escaped the claws and teeth of real lions so that the nations would know that the God of Daniel "is the living God, and he endures forever; his kingdom will never be destroyed, and his dominion has no end" (6:26). A missionary method unfolds in the evil madness of this text that God uses for good (cf. Gen 50:20).

Our God, in this passage, will glorify himself among the nations by rescuing one of his children who trusted him no matter what. He will also show us there are times and ways to exercise civil disobedience because, as Peter said in Acts 5:29, "We must obey God rather than man." For the devoted follower of King Jesus, Caesar will always lose to Christ when it comes to loyalty, obedience, and worship. *Always.*

Honor God, and Let Him Exalt You
DANIEL 6:1-4

Joel Belz has well said,

> Daniel . . . set the standard for Christians who would hold
> public office. He was serious about the work of statecraft, but
> he was even more serious about being known as a servant of
> God, determined to follow God's precepts no matter the cost.
> . . . Our society could use a few more political leaders like
> Daniel. ("Dare to Be a Daniel")

Daniel had ruled with "insight, intelligence, and wisdom" under
Nebuchadnezzar (5:11). He had a reputation as a man with "an
extraordinary spirit" (5:12), as one who had within him "a spirit of the
gods" (or "Spirit of God"; 5:14). "Insight, intelligence, and extraordinary
wisdom" (5:14) were words associated with him, continuing into
the reign of Belshazzar, the last Babylonian king. It appears Darius
shared their opinion and appointed Daniel to a position of significant
leadership. It was a good call and wise decision.

Walk in the Spirit (6:1-3)

Darius quickly set up his government with "120 satraps" or administrative districts covering the whole kingdom (v. 1). Over these smaller
regions he appointed "three administrators," three superior rulers to
whom "these satraps would be accountable . . . so that the king would
not be defrauded" (v. 2). Government corruption, it seems, is not a
modern invention!

Daniel was one of the three administrators, and to no one's surprise,
he "distinguished himself above the administrators and satraps" so that
"the king planned to set him over the whole realm" (v. 3). Daniel was a
cut above the rest. He stood head and shoulders above the others. What
was the key to Daniel's success? It was "because he had an extraordinary
spirit." This had become the consistent witness and testimony of Daniel
for some time now. In Daniel 4:8, Nebuchadnezzar saw in Daniel "a
spirit of the holy gods" (or "the Spirit of the Holy God"). He notes this
again in 4:18. The queen will reaffirm it in 5:12, and Belshazzar will
join the chorus in 5:14. Daniel's rise in power is not to be attributed so
much, if at all, to his natural ability or exceptional giftedness. It is to be
attributed to his walk with God and the work of God in his life. Daniel

was a James 3:17 man who possessed spiritual wisdom that comes from above. He was the man God had made him to be (cf. Ps 92:12-15).

Serve Faithfully (6:4)

It can get lonely at the top. Success can multiply your enemies. The blessings of the righteous can stir up the jealousy of the wicked. All three of these proverbial sayings apply directly to Daniel. Those who are blessed and honored by the Lord can expect the same trio to come their way as well.

Daniel not only possessed "an extraordinary Spirit" (v. 3), but "he was trustworthy, and no negligence or corruption was found in him" (v. 4). He reminds us of faithful Joseph in Egypt in the book of Genesis (Gen 37–50). However, the envy and jealousy of the other two administrators and the satraps moved them to take Daniel down, "trying to find a charge against Daniel regarding the kingdom." They had only one problem: "They could find no charge or corruption, for . . . no negligence or corruption was found in him." Daniel always did what he should, and he never did what he should not. As all who follow Messiah Jesus should be, he was a model worker and employee. Proverbs 20:6 says, "Many a person proclaims his own loyalty, but who can find a trustworthy person?" Well, Darius had found such a person in Daniel. By God's grace and for his glory, may it be true of you and me as well.

Be True to God Even When It May Cost You
DANIEL 6:5-15

In Ezekiel 14:14 and 20 the prophet puts Daniel in the same company as Noah and Job in terms of their righteous lives. What is about to unfold leaves no question concerning the correctness of Ezekiel's assessment of his contemporary. "Daniel's relationship with the Lord was not crisis-oriented" (Swindoll, *Daniel,* 53). It was a consistent walk with God that people saw daily. And when emergencies or crises presented themselves, Daniel was already prepared to meet them and handle them. His daily communion with God had so shaped his character that he was ready no matter what. The decision to go to the lion's den had been settled many years earlier. The cost had already been counted. To be untrue to his God was never an option!

Evil Men Will Try to Entrap a Godly Man (6:5-9)

We should expect the world and the evil one to target us as God's people. Genesis 3:15 predicted there would be continuous hostility between God's people and Satan's. We see this play out all through the Old Testament. We are seeing it play out right here in Daniel. Satan and his worldly kingdoms are in conflict with God and will remain so until the end of the age (Rev 17–19).

Jesus warned his disciples about persecution. Before he went to the cross—where the ultimate persecution took place, where the serpent struck the heel of the Seed—Jesus said the world will hate his followers and persecute us. This is because it hated him. He says in John 16:33, "You will have suffering in this world." Paul tells us in 2 Timothy 3:12, "All who want to live a godly life in Christ Jesus will be persecuted." Peter, addressing Christian exiles in 1 Peter 4:12-14, writes (with a possible allusion to the book of Daniel),

> *Dear friends, don't be surprised when the fiery ordeal comes among you to test you as if something unusual were happening to you. Instead, rejoice as you share in the sufferings of Christ, so that you may also rejoice with great joy when his glory is revealed. If you are ridiculed for the name of Christ, you are blessed, because the Spirit of glory and of God rests on you.*

Daniel's enemies were frustrated at being unable to find any act of corruption or negligence in his service to the king. He was a man of absolute integrity (cf. 1 Tim 3:1-2). His track record was spotless. However, there might be one area of his life where they could trap him: his faith and devotion to his God (v. 5). If it comes down to honoring the law of his God or the "law of the Medes and Persians" (v. 8), we know what he will choose!

So these political rivals laid aside their own differences, closed ranks, hatched a plan, and went for the jugular of the man of God. They planned to set him up. (The foreshadowing of Herod and Pilate in executing our Savior is too obvious to miss.) The conspirators came to Darius and presented a united front, beginning with the usual words of royal exaggeration, "May King Darius live forever." Of course, only one King will live forever, and his name is not Darius.

They then share their idea to honor the king, lying shamelessly in the process:

> *All the administrators of the kingdom, the prefects, satraps, advisers,*
> *and governors have agreed that the king should establish an ordinance*
> *and enforce an edict that for thirty days, anyone who petitions any god*
> *or man except you, the king, will be thrown into the lions' den.* (v. 7)

Not all were in agreement to basically make Darius god for a month! Daniel certainly wasn't, but his enemies were not going to let the truth get in the way of their wicked agenda. Their goal was not to see Daniel demoted. Their goal was to see Daniel dead.

They persuaded the king to sign their declaration into law "so that, as a law of the Medes and Persians, it is irrevocable and cannot be changed" (v. 8). Playing on the arrogance and pride of Darius worked, as it so often does with sinful men and women. Vanity is a vice that will make you act like a fool, and Darius played the fool. Verse 9 is simple and straightforward: "So King Darius signed the written edict." Flattering the king and stroking his ego worked. The trap was set.

Godly Men Will Remain Faithful to God No Matter What (6:10-15)

Christian character is not *forged* in the moment of adversity. Christian character is *revealed* in the moment of adversity. Daniel becomes aware that the document honoring Darius as the exclusive deity of the empire has been signed. His response is to do what he has always done. He obeys God rather than man and continues a pattern of spiritual devotion that has marked his life for years, a pattern his enemies knew well. He went to his home and went upstairs to the place of prayer, where his windows were open toward Jerusalem. He then got down on his knees and prayed three times that day and the following days, giving thanks to God, "just as he had done before" (v. 10). John Piper calls this "daring, defiant, disciplined prayer," noting that Daniel's public praying was not for prideful show but for public testimony. It was "a public statement about the glory of God over the glory of Darius" ("Daniel's Defiance"). Daniel did not take a month off. Daniel did not retire to a private room to pray. He had honored God in this manner all of his life in Babylon, and he would not stop now—not for a month, not for a moment. Like Paul in Philippians 3:20 and Peter in 1 Peter 2:11-12, he knew he was an exile in a world, a city, that was not his home.

We do not know the content of Daniel's prayer. I wonder if perhaps he prayed Psalm 57, a psalm of David about when he fled from Saul and hid in a cave. It was an appropriate psalm for David. It is also an appropriate psalm for Daniel. In fact, the words fit Daniel's situation perfectly! There we read,

> *Be gracious to me, God, be gracious to me,*
> *for I take refuge in you.*
> *I will seek refuge in the shadow of your wings*
> *until danger passes.*
> *I call to God Most High,*
> *to God who fulfills his purpose for me.*
> *He reaches down from heaven and saves me,*
> *challenging the one who tramples me.* Selah
> *God sends his faithful love and truth.*
> *I am surrounded by lions;*
> *I lie down among devouring lions—*
> *people whose teeth are spears and arrows,*
> *whose tongues are sharp swords.*
> *God, be exalted above the heavens;*
> *let your glory be over the whole earth.*
> *They prepared a net for my steps;*
> *I was despondent.*
> *They dug a pit ahead of me,*
> *but they fell into it!* Selah
>
> *My heart is confident, God, my heart is confident.*
> *I will sing; I will sing praises.*
> *Wake up, my soul!*
> *Wake up, harp and lyre!*
> *I will wake up the dawn.*
> *I will praise you, Lord, among the peoples;*
> *I will sing praises to you among the nations.*
> *For your faithful love is as high as the heavens;*
> *your faithfulness reaches the clouds.*
> *God, be exalted above the heavens;*
> *let your glory be over the whole earth.*

Daniel's enemies were ready and waiting. They saw what Daniel did (Dan 6:11), and they immediately brought it to the king's attention (v. 12). They even threw in a little anti-Semitism when they made their accusation ("Daniel, one of the Judean exiles"). Darius "was very displeased" at the situation and tried to find a way to deliver a man he obviously admired, appreciated, and respected (v. 14). Unfortunately, he had stepped into his own trap and was caught. His evil administrators reminded him once more (the decree is mentioned four times for emphasis and effect) of the binding nature of the law of the Medes and Persians (v. 15). When the king makes a law, even he is bound by his words. More importantly, these evil men had counted on Daniel to be true to his God, and he had been. Daniel knew that past faithfulness would be no substitute for present faithfulness. Indeed, the past had simply prepared him for the present and the future. What a witness! What a testimony to know that you can count on the man of God to be a man of God!

Trust That God Is Able to Deliver You
DANIEL 6:16-24

We have no reason to doubt that Daniel knew about Hananiah, Mishael, and Azariah and their experience with the fiery furnace of chapter 3. We now have no doubt that Daniel is of the same constitution and conviction as they when they said,

> *Our God whom we serve is able to deliver us from the burning fiery furnace [for Daniel, from the lion's den], and he will deliver us out of your hand, O king. But if not, be it known to you, O King, that we will not serve your gods or worship [what] you have set up.* (Dan 3:17-18 ESV)

The three Hebrews told Nebuchadnezzar that their allegiance to God always trumped government or any other idol. Daniel tells Darius the same thing. Fidelity to God is not subject to debate or vote (cf. Acts 4:19-20). For all four Hebrew men, this issue was settled in their hearts long before they faced their challenge.

We Can Rest in God's Plan (6:16-18)

Much to his regret Darius commanded that Daniel be thrown "into the lions' den" (v. 16). The den was probably a pit with an opening at the top. As Daniel was about to be thrown into the pit, his friend, the king, spoke to Daniel: "May your God, whom you continually serve, rescue you!" Stephen Miller notes, "Darius' concern for his friend is touching. . . . The words express the king's hope" (*Daniel,* 185). Daniel, however, was not resting in the king's concern or his hope. He was resting in the providence and sovereignty of his God.

Daniel was cast into the lion's den, and "a stone was brought and placed over the mouth of the den" (v. 17). I guess this was to be sure the eighty-year-old man would not jump out! The king also sealed Daniel's tomb "with his own signet ring and with the signet rings of his nobles, so that nothing in regard to Daniel could be changed." We can only imagine the joy of these lords attending this "Rose Garden" ceremony and signing.

Darius did not share in their delight. Verse 18 informs us, "Then the king went to his palace and spent the night fasting. No diversions [NIV, "entertainment"] were brought to him, and he could not sleep." No doubt Darius's lords were out partying. Not so for the king. No food. No partying. No music. He knew he had been played, and it had cost him the life of his loyal friend. Ligon Duncan points out,

> Of course, this passage bears an uncanny resemblance to Matthew 26:65-66, where we read, "Pilate said to them, 'You have a guard, go, make it as secure as you know how,' and they went and made the grave secure, and along with the guard, they set a seal on the stone." Just as Daniel was sealed in the lion's den, so also Christ was sealed in the tomb, and this was the petty human ruler's way to seal the fate of both of these great servants of the Lord. And in both cases, that human sealing led to greater glory for God, when He brought Daniel up out of the pit and He raised Christ up out of the tomb.
>
> It's not surprising that the early Church saw in Daniel in the lion's den, a prefiguring of the resurrection of the Lord, for as Daniel was brought out of a den that had been sealed by the official rings of those in power, so was the Lord Jesus Christ raised from a tomb which had been sealed by those officials with their rings of power. ("Daniel in the Lion's Den")

We Can Be Certain of God's Power (6:19-24)

Like Mary Magdalene and the other Mary in Matthew 28:1, Darius went "at the first light of dawn" (v. 19) to the tomb holding what might remain of Daniel's body. As he approached the den of lions, "he cried out in anguish, . . . 'Daniel, servant of the living God, . . . has your God, whom you continually serve, been able to rescue you from the lions?'" (v. 20). The doubt in his voice is unmistakable. He did not expect to hear a thing other than the satisfied purring of lions following their supper.

Suddenly, and no doubt to his joyful surprise, Daniel speaks (vv. 21-22)! This is the only time Daniel's words are recorded in the entire chapter. We might playfully paraphrase Daniel like this:

> Good morning, my king. I hope things are going well with you and that you enjoyed a good night's sleep. I did! I slept like a little lamb with your lions as my guests. Their quiet purring put me right to sleep, and their warm bodies and fur kept me from being cold all night. Such sweet, cute cats! Oh, I also had a very special guest show up. "My God sent his angel and shut the lions' mouths" (v. 22). Why I did not even get a lick from their tongue—not one. "They haven't harmed me." They did not touch one gray hair on my head. Of course, you should know the reason. I honored my God, and I never did anything wrong to you. I put the whole situation in the hands of my King, and this is what he did. I trusted him either way, and I will continue to do so as long as I live. Now, would you like to come down and join me?

Once again I appreciate the insight and perspective of Ligon Duncan at this point:

> Daniel is not claiming to be sinless, Daniel is not claiming to never have done anything wrong, but Daniel is saying, in the heat of the moment, I chose God, and I'm innocent before Him. I didn't do anything wrong in this circumstance before God. And furthermore, O King, I didn't do anything wrong to you. Your henchmen, these beauracrats, have accused me of not having respect for you. That couldn't be further from the truth, but no one has precedent or priority over my God, and therefore I have done nothing wrong to you and I've done nothing wrong to Him. ("Daniel in the Lion's Den")

Well, Darius did not join Daniel in the lions' den, but some others took his place (v. 24). Those who "maliciously accused Daniel," along with their families, were thrown into the lions' den and killed even before they "reached the bottom of the den." Sinclair Ferguson once more provides a helpful word at this point:

> In a fallen and sinful world there is a somber side to the salvation of God's people. The deliverance of Eve's seed is always accompanied by the bruising of the head of the

serpent (Gen. 3:15). Christ delivers those who were subject to a lifelong fear of death by destroying the one who had the power of death (Heb. 2:14-15). The dark side to Daniel's deliverance is the judgment that falls on those who had sought to destroy the kingdom of God. They and their entire families, even wives and children, were cast into the den of lions and immediately attacked and devoured. Herodotus informs us that such punishment of entire families was meted out according to Persian Law. It was a terrible end. Their gods were unable to deliver them from the lions, whereas Daniel's God had delivered him. The One who was in Daniel was stronger than the one who was in the world (cf. 1 John 4:4).

The closing verses of this chapter provide an appropriate climax to the first section of the book as well as to the miracle of Daniel's deliverance. Darius, whatever his ultimate spiritual condition, confessed the supreme authority of "*the God of Daniel*" (v. 26). (*Daniel*, 130)

Recognize God Will Use You to Make His Name Famous among the Nations
DANIEL 6:25-28

Bob Fyall makes a number of helpful observations about how these verses fit into the book as a whole when he writes,

> In Chapters 2, 3 and 4, Nebuchadnezzar had praised Daniel's God in an increasingly reverent way. In Chapter 5 there had been no such praise from Belshazzar who had already passed the point of no return. Here Darius virtually encapsulates the theology of the whole book in a song of praise which summarizes what God has done in the last chapters and points forward to the theology of history about to be unfolded in the second part of the book. (*Daniel*, 91)

God Can Cause Unbelievers to Acknowledge His Greatness (6:25-26)

Darius has clearly been impacted by God's miraculous deliverance of Daniel. In words reminiscent of the Psalms, and in particular Psalm 2, this unbelieving ruler writes "to those of every people, nation, and language who live on the whole earth" (v. 25). Once more the language of Daniel anticipates the glorious eschatological missionary promise of

Revelation 5 and 7. The decree or letter begins with words of blessing, "May your prosperity abound." The king then quickly follows with a command or warning, "that in all [his] royal dominion, people must tremble in fear before the God of Daniel" (v. 26). The declaration accomplishes at least two important purposes. First, it recognizes the greatness, even the superiority, of Israel's God over all would-be rivals. And second, it cancels out the irrevocable edict of 6:6-9 (Hill, "Daniel," 127). Once again we see the truth of Proverbs 21:1: "A king's heart is like channeled water in the LORD's hand: He directs it wherever he chooses."

God Can Even Use Unbelievers to Proclaim His Glory (6:26-28)

The content of the decree is in verses 26-27. It is a theological doxology that takes note of God's greatness universally (v. 26) and personally (v. 27). As to his nature, he is the living and eternal God. As to his sovereignty, his kingdom will not be destroyed or brought to an end (v. 26). He is universally unparalleled and without rival.

On the personal level he is a delivering and rescuing God. He is not limited spatially, for he works his signs and wonders, his mighty and supernatural acts, "in the heavens and on the earth." In the most immediate context, just look to Daniel, whom he has rescued "from the power of the lions" (v. 27).

Once again God honors his faithful servant. Just as he blessed and honored Daniel under the Babylonians, Nebuchadnezzar and Belshazzar, he does so again under the Medo-Persians and Darius (that is, Cyrus the Persian; v. 28). The truth of James 4:10 rings forth again, "Humble yourselves before the Lord, and he will exalt you." The New Living Translation says, "He will lift you up in honor."

Conclusion: How Does the Text Point to Christ?

Throughout the Bible, especially the Old Testament, God uses typology to point us to a coming deliverer, a rescuer, in fulfillment of the first gospel promise in Genesis 3:15. Sometimes our Lord uses events like the Passover in Exodus 12. Other times he uses institutions like the temple and the sacrificial system. And still other times he uses individuals like Adam, Abraham, Moses, David, and Daniel. In the messianic Psalm 22, the righteous sufferer proclaims in verse 21, "Save me from the lion's mouth." God indeed saved Messiah Jesus from the mouth of the lion of death by his glorious resurrection. In like manner he saved Daniel from a lion's attack when early in the morning, "at the first light of dawn"

(6:19), Darius arrived at what could be described as Daniel's tomb, only to discover he was not dead; he was alive!

Lest you think I am guilty of overreading the text, let me point you to Tim Keller's encouragement for us all to develop an instinct for seeing Jesus in all of Scripture. If it is true that the Bible is not about me but about Jesus, "the source and perfecter of our faith" (Heb 12:2), then we are justified to see him here in Daniel. He illustrates this instinct beautifully:

> Jesus is the *true and better Adam*, who passed the test in the garden, His garden—a much tougher garden—and whose obedience is imputed to us.
>
> Jesus is the *true and better Abel*, who though innocently slain, has blood that cries out, not for our condemnation, but for our acquittal.
>
> Jesus is the *true and better Abraham*, who answered the call of God to leave all the comfortable and familiar and go into the void not knowing whither He went.
>
> Jesus is the *true and better Isaac*, who was not just offered up by His Father on the mount, but was truly sacrificed for us all while God said to Abraham, "Now I know you love Me because you did not withhold your son, your only son, whom you love from Me." Now we at the foot of the cross can say to God, "Now we know that You love me because You did not withhold Your Son, Your only Son whom You love, from me."
>
> Jesus is the *true and better Jacob*, who wrestled and took the blow of justice we deserve so we, like Jacob, only receive the wounds of grace that wake us up and discipline us.
>
> Jesus is the *true and better Joseph*, who is at the right hand of the king and forgives those who betrayed and sold him and uses his power to save them.
>
> Jesus is the *true and better Moses*, who stands in the gap between the people and the Lord and who mediates a new covenant.
>
> Jesus is the *true and better Rock of Moses* who, struck with the rod of God's justice, now gives us water in the desert.
>
> Jesus is the *true and better Job*—He's the truly innocent sufferer who then intercedes for and saves His stupid friends. . . .
>
> Jesus is the *true and better David*, whose victory becomes His people's victory though they never lifted a stone to accomplish it themselves.

Jesus is the *true and better Esther*, who didn't just risk losing an earthly palace, but lost the ultimate heavenly one, who didn't just risk His life, but gave His life, who didn't say, "If I perish, I perish," but said, "When I perish, I will perish for them to save My people."

Jesus is the *true and better Jonah*, who was cast out into the storm so we could be brought in.

He's the real Passover Lamb. He's the true temple, the true prophet, the true priest, the true king, the true sacrifice, the true lamb, the true light, the true bread. ("What Is Gospel-Centered Ministry?")

Indeed Jesus is all of these things. And to them we may rightly add, Jesus is the *true and better Daniel*, who having been lowered into a lion's den of death, emerges early the next morning alive and vindicated by his God.

Reflect and Discuss

1. Why do you think this story connects so much with the hearts and imaginations of those who hear or read it? Why do you think it is so hard for some to believe?
2. What can we learn from Daniel about how to live faithfully in the midst of a culture that does not honor God?
3. What characteristics make Daniel stand out and allow him to ascend to high leadership positions in the kingdom?
4. Why should Christians who are serving God faithfully expect opposition? How does Daniel handle this opposition?
5. What does it mean for one's faith to be crisis oriented, and how does it contrast with Daniel's faith?
6. How can you prepare now for when opposition will come? What instruction does Jesus give about persecution?
7. Daniel's faithfulness to God led him to disobey the earthly king. In what kinds of issues should we be prepared to serve God rather than man?
8. God's power is put on display in this passage. Who and what are shown ultimately to be under the authority of Daniel's God?
9. In what sense is this a missionary text? How does it point us to the nations?
10. How do Daniel's situation and character remind you of Jesus?

Is Anyone Really in Control? Yes! God Is!

DANIEL 7:1-28

Main Idea: God reigns over all nations and will finally defeat his enemies through the coming kingdom of his Son, who took on flesh in Jesus Christ.

I. **God Is Sovereign over the Nations (7:1-8).**
   - A. He reveals what he chooses to show us (7:1).
   - B. He raises up whom he chooses for power (7:2-8).

II. **God Is Sovereign over His Kingdom (7:9-14).**
   - A. He is sovereign because of his eternality and purity (7:9-10).
   - B. He is sovereign with his sentence and patience (7:11-12).
   - C. He is sovereign in his man and plan (7:13-14).

III. **God Is Sovereign in His Judgment (7:15-28).**
   - A. God's people will receive an eternal kingdom that will last forever (7:15-18).
   - B. God's people will suffer in an earthly kingdom that will last only a short time (7:19-26).
   - C. God's people will be given a universal kingdom that will last forever (7:27-28).

In the sci-fi thriller *Aliens* (1986), a rescue team from Earth faces off against hostile alien monsters that inflict serious carnage on the team. Amazingly, a small girl named Newt has lived for months on the planet as the lone survivor of a prior mission. After a particularly bad encounter with the aliens, Newt informs leader Ellen Ripley (played by Sigourney Weaver) that the team needs to quickly get back to a safe place. Why? Her words are classic and memorable: "We better get back because it will be dark soon. And they mostly come at night . . . mostly." Newt is right. Monsters mostly come at night . . . mostly. They come out at night when it is dark. They come out at night when we lie in our beds. They come out at night when we sleep in "dreams with visions," as the prophet Daniel would quickly affirm.

Daniel 7 has been called "the most comprehensive and detailed prophecy of future events to be found anywhere in the Old Testament"

(Walvoord, *Daniel*, 145). It is a connecting chapter that overlays and ties Daniel 1–6 with Daniel 7–12. Beginning in Daniel 2:4 and going through Daniel 7:28, the book is written in Aramaic. Before and after those verses, the book is written in Hebrew. Thus, the Aramaic section of Daniel begins with a vision given to Nebuchadnezzar in chapter 2 and ends with a parallel vision given to Daniel in chapter 7. Daniel 1–6 is narrative and personal. Daniel 7–12 is apocalyptic and cosmic. These latter chapters, like the former, emphasize the absolute sovereignty of God over all things. And chapters 7–12 give us insight concerning the future as God graciously reveals to us, through Daniel, his plans for world history and the end of time. Dan Duncan is correct:

> From chapter 7 on, the book is very different. It doesn't continue the chronology of events, but reverts back in time to a series of visions that Daniel had. It's not history; it is prophecy. In a sense, the first half of the book gives the credentials of the prophet, the reliability of the messenger. The second half gives his message. Now, the message of chapter 7 through chapter 12 is really not new. . . . It's the message that God is sovereign. ("God and Monsters, Dan 7:1-14")

God is indeed sovereign. Daniel 7 makes this truth abundantly clear as it provides something of a panoramic preview of coming attractions from the time of Daniel until that day when time is no more.

The chapter naturally divides into three movements or sections (vv. 1-8,9-14,15-28). Ideas of "seeing" and "looking" dominate throughout. In the vision of chapter 2, we see history as man sees it. In chapter 7, we see history as God sees it. The perspectives are different.

God Is Sovereign over the Nations
DANIEL 7:1-8

The Bible uses various genres and literary styles to teach us God's truth. Daniel 7–12 is primarily what we call apocalyptic literature, which is marked by visions and vivid word pictures. David Helm says, "Story-telling gives way to movie-watching" (*Daniel for You*, 117). Dale Davis is helpful when he writes,

> I would say that biblical apocalyptic is a sort of prophecy that seeks to enlighten and encourage a people despised and cast

off by the world with a vision of the God who will come to impose his kingdom on the wreckage and rebellion of human history—and it communicates this message through the use of wild, scary, imaginative, bizarre and head-scratching imagery. (*Message of Daniel,* 93)

Those who are visually oriented find this form of communication enjoyable. Children who are immersed in the world of video games may identify with it more easily than their parents!

So the sovereignty of God is going to be taught via sci-fi. Truth will be conveyed symbolically through wild, crazy, and strange imagery. There is real stuff behind the symbols, but it will be a challenge to find the right keys to unlock these spectacular scenes that flash before us.

He Reveals What He Chooses to Show Us (7:1)

Daniel provides a historical marker for us: "In the first year of King Belshazzar of Babylon." The story of Belshazzar has already been conveyed in Daniel 5. It was not a pretty picture, as his drunken orgy ends with his death and the fall of the Babylonian Empire to the Medes and Persians. The first year of Belshazzar's reign was around 553 BC. Daniel would have been in his mid-sixties and Belshazzar in his mid-thirties (Miller, *Daniel,* 194).

At this particular time God chose to give his divine revelation to Daniel in dreams and visions at night "as he was lying in his bed." Believing, knowing, that this was from God, "he wrote down the dream and told the sum of the matter" (ESV). We are indebted to Daniel for preserving what God showed him on this particular night "in his mind." We are the beneficiaries. God revealed, and Daniel wrote. That is a good description of how our Lord delivers his divine, infallible, and inerrant revelation.

He Raises Up Whom He Chooses for Power (7:2-8)

These verses record what could be called "the rise of the beasts." Sinclair Ferguson notes that what we have here

> is essentially a book of pictures, appealing to our senses.
> We are meant to see, hear, and smell the strange beasts
> that appear throughout this chapter. We are meant to be
> overwhelmed as Daniel was. (*Daniel,* 135)

Daniel first sees that "the four winds of heaven stirred up the great sea" (v. 2). That the four winds of the compass (north, south, east, and west) are here referred to as the "winds of heaven" teaches us this is God's doing. "The great sea" should be understood symbolically as the raging chaos, confusion, and conflict among the nations of the world. Isaiah 17:12 says, "Ah! The roar of many peoples—they roar like the roaring of the seas. The raging of the nations—they rage like the rumble of rushing water" (cf. Job 41:31; Rev 17:15).

Verses 3-8 reveal what Daniel saw: "Four huge beasts came up from the sea, each different from the other" (v. 3). Let's quickly examine each one. Chapter 2 and our understanding of it will be helpful in this interpretation because the two visions are parallel. Interestingly, allowing an animal to serve as a symbol for a nation continues in our day. For example, Britain uses the lion, Russia the bear, and America the eagle.

The first beast "was like a lion but had eagle's wings" (v. 4). This is Nebuchadnezzar and Babylon, which we can tell both from the allusion and from the fact that both Jeremiah and Ezekiel compare Nebuchadnezzar and Babylon to a lion and an eagle (Jer 4:7; 49:19; 50:44; Ezek 17:3,11-12). Babylon was ferocious like a lion and swift like an eagle. However, "its wings were torn off" (Dan 7:4; ESV, "plucked off"), most likely a reference to Nebuchadnezzar's humbling insanity in 4:28-33. Then the lion "was lifted up from the ground, set on its feet like a man, and given a human mind." The phrases "it was lifted up" and "the mind of a man was given to it" (ESV) are what we call the divine passive, indicating both were the activity of God. He is the implied agent of action. Nebuchadnezzar was restored from his beastly existence and behavior by God (4:34-37).

Daniel's "jungle book" continues as his first scene fades off the apocalyptic screen and a new one takes its place. He sees a second beast, a bear (v. 5). "It was raised up on one side" (again, by God) and had "three ribs in its mouth between its teeth." God then tells it, "Get up! Gorge yourself on flesh." This beast is Medo-Persia. Being raised up on one side may describe the dominance of the Persians over the Medes. Three ribs in its mouth tells us "it was not fasting" (Davis, *Message of Daniel*, 94). Dogmatism is unwarranted in identifying the three ribs. However, James Montgomery Boice offers a plausible possibility when he points out,

> Cyrus, the Median-Persian King, and his son Cambyses
> conquered (1) the Lydian Kingdom in Asia Minor, which

fell to Cyrus in 546 BC; (2) the Chaldean Empire, which he
overthrew in 539 BC; and (3) the kingdom of Egypt, which fell
to Cambyses in 525. (*Daniel,* 76)

Stephen Miller also suggests the three ribs represent "Babylon (539
BC), Lydia (546 BC), and Egypt (525 BC)" (*Daniel,* 199). On the other
hand, E. J. Young's suggestion (following John Calvin) that the three
ribs represent "the insatiable nature of the beast" is certainly a safe interpretation (*Prophecy of Daniel,* 145).

The third beast, in verse 6, looks "like a leopard with four wings
of a bird" and "four heads." It is a powerful beast because "it was given
dominion." This is clearly Greece and Alexander the Great. With speed
and agility that was unprecedented, he conquered the world of his day—
all the way to India—only to die suddenly at the age of thirty-three.
Stephen Miller provides helpful insight on both the symbolism and
what transpired following Alexander's death. The accuracy of biblical
prophecy is truly amazing!

> In Scripture "heads" may represent rulers or governments
> (e.g., 2:38; Isa. 7:8-9; Rev. 13:3,12), and that is the case with the
> leopard's four heads. Daniel predicted that this one empire
> would ultimately evolve into four kingdoms, and this is exactly
> what occurred. Alexander died in 323 B.C., and after much
> internal struggle his generals carved the kingdom into four
> parts: (1) Antipater, and later Cassander, gained control of
> Greece and Macedonia; (2) Lysimachus ruled Thrace and
> a large part of Asia Minor; (3) Seleucus I Nicator governed
> Syria, Babylon, and much of the Middle East (all of Asia
> except Asia Minor and Palestine); and (4) Ptolemy I Soter
> controlled Egypt and Palestine. A quadripartite character is
> definitely ascribed to the Greek Empire in the next chapter
> (cp. 8:8 with 8:21-22), and it is reasonable to interpret the
> leopard's "four heads" in light of that clear teaching. (Miller,
> *Daniel,* 200)

The fourth and final beast is described in verses 7-8. This beast is
the most "frightening and dreadful" of all. It is "incredibly strong, with
large iron teeth. It devoured and crushed, and it trampled with its feet
whatever was left." And it was of a different nature altogether from the
other three beasts. It had ten horns, which convey at minimum great and

complete power (cf. 2:40-42). This beast is without question the Roman Empire, and yet I believe it is also more. Verse 8, and the additional commentary concerning this beast in verses 19-26, drive me to such an understanding. Verse 8 tells us an eleventh horn, a little horn, emerges from the ten. It begins small but grows to have both great intelligence (i.e., the eyes of a man) and a big mouth. All of this brings Revelation 13 to mind. We will expand our study of this beast shortly, but James Boice seems to be on track when he says,

> This seems to be the first biblical reference to the individual later described in the Bible as the Antichrist. He appears in 2 Thessalonians 2 as "the man of lawlessness . . . doomed for destruction" (v. 3) and is seen again in Revelation. (*Daniel*, 76)

Daniel 2, 7, and also 8 overlap and parallel one another. A visual chart helps us see that relationship more clearly.

Correlation of Dreams and Visions in Daniel[4]				
	Image Chapter 2	Beasts Chapter 7	Beasts Chapter 8	Kingdoms Represented
The Times of the Gentiles Luke 21:24	Head of fine gold	Like a lion with eagle's wings		Babylon 626–539 BC
	Chest and arms of silver	Like a bear	Ram with two horns	Medo-Persia 539–330 BC
	Belly and thighs of bronze	Like a leopard with four wings and four heads	Male goat with one great horn, four horns, and little horn	Greece 330–63 BC
	Legs of iron, feet of iron and clay	Incomparable beast with ten horns and little horn		Rome 63 BC–?
	Stone that becomes a great mountain	Messiah (Son of Man) and saints receive the kingdom		Kingdom of God

[4] Slightly adapted from Criswell, *The Believer's Study Bible*, 1180.

God Is Sovereign over His Kingdom
DANIEL 7:9-14

Daniel saw quite a show in verses 3-8. However, he has not seen anything yet! As terrifying as those verses were, verses 9-14 are more awesome, more glorious, and certainly more comforting. God is sovereign over the nations because, as we now see, he is sovereign over his kingdom.

Verses 9-14 contain three scenes that follow in rapid-fire succession. If Daniel 7 is, as many say, "the single most important chapter of the book" (Miller, *Daniel,* 191), verses 9-14 are almost certainly the most important verses in Daniel and some of the most important verses in the whole Bible. They are important theologically. They are important eschatologically. And they are important Christologically.

He Is Sovereign Because of His Eternality and Purity (7:9-10)

Daniel continues watching (see vv. 1-2,4,6-7,11,13,21). This scene is radically different from the previous ones. He does not see a beast in it. He sees thrones and "the Ancient of Days," who takes a seat on his throne (cf. 1 Kgs 22:19; Rev 4:4). Only Daniel calls God the Ancient of Days. This is God the Father on his eternal and universal throne. As the Ancient of Days he is eternal, not old. He is wise, not senile! He is a big God, bigger than even Daniel realized, and bigger than the petty beast kingdoms of this world. The following descriptions make that crystal clear.

- "His clothing was white like snow"—speaks of his holiness, purity, and righteousness.
- "The hair of his head [was] like whitest wool"—speaks of his eternality, purity, and wisdom. He has always existed, and he is wise beyond all comparison.
- "His throne was flaming fire"—speaks of purifying and righteous judgment.
- "Its wheels were blazing fire"—tells us there are no spatial limitations or restrictions on his judgment. He sees everything, and he is everywhere present.
- "A river of fire was flowing, coming out from his presence"— reinforces the two previous ideas and conveys the righteous fury and wrath of his judgment. Psalm 97:3 says, "Fire goes before him and burns up his foes on every side."

- "Thousands upon thousands served him; ten thousand times ten thousand stood before him"—sounds like Revelation 5:11 and is a reference to angels.

Before this awesome and imposing King, court is called into session "and the books were opened." The Ancient of Days does everything by the book. His judgment, as always, will be fair and equitable. There is no partiality, not a hint of unfairness. This is true for his judgment of everyone, beginning with the beast.

He Is Sovereign with His Sentence and Patience (7:11-12)

The little horn (v. 8) is still mouthing off as the vision reverts back to him. This arrogant braggart and his boasting are framed or sandwiched by two God-focused poems (vv. 9-10,13-14) (Pierce, *Daniel*, 125). In verse 11, suddenly and without elaboration, he is taken out: "The beast was killed and its body destroyed and given over to the burning fire" (cf. Rev 19:19-21; 20:10). Turn out the lights on the beast. Game over! It is that quick. It is that simple.

In contrast to the fourth beast, the others had "their dominion . . . removed, but an extension of life was granted to them for a certain period of time" (v. 12). Sidney Greidanus notes that Babylon, Medo-Persia, and Greece, even after losing their dominion, continued to exist and live as part of the kingdom that conquered them. They were shadows of themselves, but they were still there, albeit in a much diminished sense. God was more gracious and patient with them, as he has been with many other kingdoms throughout history. Not so for the Roman Empire, as it comes to its fullest and greatest expression in the little horn, the antichrist. "When God judges the little horn, the last remnant of the Roman Empire will be annihilated" (Greidanus, *Preaching Christ from Daniel*, 241).

He Is Sovereign in His Man and Plan (7:13-14)

Two persons take center stage in this night vision: "one like a son of man" and "the Ancient of Days." These two verses were considered important by the authors of the New Testament, being referenced numerous times, and they are loaded with theological significance. Daniel sees someone "coming with the clouds of heaven," a clear indication of divinity, and a Christophany as we will see (see also Exod 16:10; 19:9; 24:16; 34:5; Num 11:25; Pss 97:2; 104:3; Isa 19:1; Nah 1:3). "He approached the Ancient of Days [i.e., God the Father] and was escorted before him." The one like a son of man is then given by the Ancient of Days a universal and eternal kingdom. Verse 14 should be read carefully and slowly so that its impact and weight is fully felt and taken in. The eternal and universal kingdom of God is given to "one like a son of man" who comes in divine manifestation "with the clouds of heaven."

So the question begging to be asked and answered is, Who is this son of man? A nonexhaustive list of possible candidates includes Daniel, Israel, Michael, Gabriel, Judas Maccabee, faithful Israel, and glorified Israel. However, none of these is satisfactory. Furthermore, Jesus Christ himself tells us who the son of man is. It is he! The title *Son of Man* was Jesus's favorite self-designated title and was used almost exclusively by him (see also Acts 7:56; Rev 1:13). The title appears sixty-nine times in the Synoptic Gospels and twelve times in John. In Mark 10:45, Jesus weds the title to the Suffering Servant of Isaiah 53 and thereby redefines the concept of Messiah. In Mark 14:62, he weds the title to Psalm 110 and the King/Priest portrait of Messiah. Concerning the title *Son of Man*, Sinclair Ferguson says,

> The expression "Son of Man" appears to be the virtual equivalent of "man," but when "One like the Son of Man" appears, the title has particular rather than general significance. This is the True Man in contrast to the man-become-beast in the earlier elements of the vision. This is the one who is able to stand in the presence of the God whose throne is made of the fire of His judgment. This is the one who is worthy to receive "dominion and glory and a kingdom, that all peoples, nations, and languages should serve Him. His dominion is an everlasting dominion" (v. 14). This True Man is all that humans as God's image were meant to be but failed to be. (*Daniel*, 144-45)

Christ was given this glorious kingdom following his work of atonement when he ascended back to heaven. However, Jesus himself declares in Matthew 24:29-31 that the full manifestation and realization of this kingdom will occur when he comes again "on the clouds of heaven with power and great glory." Jesus Christ did not hesitate to identify himself with the Son of Man in Daniel 7, and neither should we! A vision

> that began like a nightmare with monsters coming out of the sea, ends happily and hopefully with a Man coming out of

heaven whom God crowns sovereign over the world! (Duncan, "Daniel")

God Is Sovereign in His Judgment
DANIEL 7:15-28

Sometimes even a vision of the greatness and glory of God is still not enough to overcome our anxieties, concerns, and troubled hearts. I take some comfort in knowing I am not alone. Daniel had the same struggle! I guess we are in good company when moments of distress afflict and overwhelm us.

Verses 15-28 bring the vision of Daniel to a close. It easily divides into three parts: verses 15-18 ("my spirit was deeply distressed within me"), verses 19-27 ("Then I wanted to be clear . . ."), and verse 28 ("This is the end of the account"). Because verse 27 stands in contrast with verses 23-26, I will join it to verse 28 in our teaching outline.

God's People Will Receive an Eternal Kingdom That Will Last Forever (7:15-18)

All Daniel had seen to this point deeply distressed him (ESV, "my spirit within me was anxious") and "the visions in my mind terrified me" (v. 15). He "approached one of those who were standing by" (probably an angel) and asked for some help. The angel obliged and provided an interpretation (v. 16). As we noted earlier, the four beasts are four kings/kingdoms "who will rise from the earth" (v. 17). They stand in contrast to the Son of Man who comes down from heaven (v. 13). Their temporal kingdom (v. 12) also stands in contrast to the kingdom of the saints of God, here identified as "the holy ones of the Most High" (v. 18). These holy ones "will receive the kingdom and possess it forever, yes, forever and ever." Once again we see the biblical principle of solidarity with our head. We share in what the Ancient of Days gives the Son of Man. The use of the title Son of Man certainly points in that direction. I cannot improve on the words of Sinclair Ferguson at this point:

> The One like the Son of Man is related in some special way to "the saints of the Most High" so that they share in His dominion.
>
> The correctness of this view is underlined by the way in which the One like the Son of Man here appears to be all that

Adam failed to be. Adam was a historical individual according to Scripture, but he was also an individual whose actions carried unique consequences for others. Paul expounds this in great detail (Rom. 5:12-21; I Cor. 15:47ff.). In and through Adam's fall, sin and death came to all who followed. His actions had consequences for a whole species. So, too, with the One like the Son of Man. His conquest means that all those who belong to Him share in the victory. This teaching is also examined in Hebrews (Heb. 2:5-18). Taking up the words of Psalm 2 that all things are under human dominion (cf. Gen. 1:28), the author reflects on the contrast between the promise and the reality. We do not yet see everything in subjection to ourselves, but, says Hebrews, "We see Jesus, who was made a little lower than the angels, for the suffering of death crowned with glory and honor, that He, by the grace of God, might taste death for everyone" (Heb. 2:9). This is what Daniel perceived so vividly, if puzzlingly, in chapter 7. The coronation of the One like the Son of Man is the assurance that those who belong to Him will share in His dominion (cf. Rev. 20:6). (*Daniel*, 147–48).

God's People Will Suffer in an Earthly Kingdom That Will Last Only a Short Time (7:19-26)

In verses 19-20 Daniel expresses his desire to know about the fourth terrifying beast of verses 7-8. The two descriptions are virtually identical. In verse 21 he sees the little horn warring against God's holy ones (saints) and defeating them (see Rev 13:7). He was able to do so until the Ancient of Days stepped in and rescued them, giving them the kingdom in the process (v. 22).

Verses 23-26 describe this fourth beast, who is also the final beast. He is Rome and more, as Revelation 13:1-10 clearly teaches. He is an incredibly powerful and vicious king/kingdom who will devour, trample, and crush (v. 23), rise and subdue (v. 24), speak against the Most High, oppress the saints, and intend to change the times and law (v. 25). He is different from any and all other kingdoms (v. 23-24). However, his reign is a limited one—"time, times, and half a time" (v. 25)—and he will be decisively judged and destroyed by God in the end (v. 26). Some specifics of this vision must remain a mystery (the ten kings of v. 24 and the three kings put down in the same verse). Again, I am greatly aided by the insights of Sinclair Ferguson:

Ten horns grew out of the beast. If the beast represents the Roman Empire, then the ten horns are best taken as the continuation of the spirit that was so powerfully expressed in that empire. The little horn arises in this context and engages in hostile activity against three of the horns.

Earlier Protestant commentators often saw a reflection of the little horn in the power of the papacy. Calvin, on the other hand, saw its fulfillment in the Roman Empire itself. In Daniel's vision, however, the little horn represents the final consummation of evil. It belongs to the final days. Therefore, it ought not be given a specific identification in any historical figure. Notice, however, that the little horn emerges in the context of the beast and the ten horns. It should not surprise us that there will be continual expressions of the characteristics of the little horn that will reach their apex in appearances of the little horn in the last days as described in Daniel's conclusion. Nevertheless, it is not surprising that many dictators and empire-builders have been identified with the little horn and have shared some of its worst features. We have been told that the Antichrist will come in the final days, but that does not preclude our recognizing that many antichrists have already strutted across the pages of history (1 John 2:18). (*Daniel*, 147–48)

Antichrists and "the antichrist" blaspheme God, persecute God's people, and are lawbreakers and disrupters of God's good design (see Dan 2:21). They deify themselves and turn the social order into godless chaos. This reaches a climax when the "beast coming up out of the sea" in Revelation 13 emerges. He has and has had many forerunners, but he will top them all. However, his reign will quickly come to an end, and when it does, no human like him will ever appear again!

God's People Will Be Given a Universal Kingdom That Will Last Forever (7:27-28)

Daniel is told for a second time that saints will be given a universal and eternal kingdom (v. 27). The God "Most High" will see to it. Piddly despots like Antiochus Epiphanes come and go (175–164 BC). Madmen like Nero are here today and gone tomorrow (AD 54–68). Lunatics like Hitler have a reign of terror only for a season (1933–45). Antichrist, the final ruler emerging from the sea, will have his day for only three and a half years. In marvelous and striking contrast, God's kingdom "will be an everlasting kingdom, and all rulers will serve and obey him" (v. 27), they will obey the Son of Man. This is good news and the "end of the matter" (v. 28 ESV).

However, it is a lot to take in! I think we can readily understand why Daniel says, "My thoughts terrified me greatly, and my face turned pale [lit. 'my brightness changed on me'], but I kept the matter to myself" (cf. Eccl 12:13; Jer 51:64). Perhaps Daniel's perplexity might be explained like this: I know a great and wonderful and eternal kingdom is on the way, but there is a long and hard road of suffering before it arrives. Battles will be lost, but the war will be won when the Son of Man comes. Wow! What a wonderful and hope-giving promise!

Conclusion: Where Is Christ in This Text?

This is an easy question to answer in this text. He is front and center in 7:13-14 as the Son of Man, the divine-human person, who receives the universal kingdom from his Father, "the Ancient of Days." Revelation 5:9-10 and 7:9-13 worshipfully draw from this glorious vision in Daniel. Universal worship of the Son of Man is on the way!

Yet there is more. Who destroys the beast (Dan 7:11) but the Son of Man in his majestic second coming (Rev 19:11-21)? The deathblow was delivered in his first advent when he cried, "It is finished," from a bloody cross (John 19:30). Therefore even before he ascended to his Father (Luke 24:50-53; Acts 1:6-11), Jesus could declare in Matthew 28:18, "All authority has been given to me in heaven and on earth." So the beast, and Satan who works behind him and through him, may "oppress the holy ones of the Most High" for a season (Dan 7:25), but it will come to an end. Until then, realize that the Son of God became the Son of Man so that he might identify with us and comfort us. Charles Spurgeon said it well: "As surely as He overcame, and triumphed once for you, so surely you that love his name, shall triumph in him too" (*Sermons on the Book of Daniel*, 154).

Reflect and Discuss

1. Why do you think Daniel's readers would have been comforted to hear this message of God's sovereignty?
2. Explain in your own words what apocalyptic literature is and how we should interpret it in Scripture.

3. What do each of the beasts suggest about the strengths of their respective kingdoms? What weaknesses do these images suggest?

4. How is God shown to be sovereign even over the beasts (i.e., kings and their kingdoms) in verses 4-8?

5. Summarize the importance of Daniel 7:9-14 to theology (doctrine of God), Christology (doctrine of Christ), and eschatology (doctrine of the end times).

6. How does the description of God in 7:9-10 show his superiority over the beasts?

7. What does the last beast symbolize, other than just the Roman Empire? How does that help us apply this passage to our contemporary context?

8. What evidence in the Bible is there that the Son of Man should be identified with Jesus?

9. What words of comfort and promise does this give God's people?

10. Based on this and other relevant passages of Scripture, describe the nature and character of the antichrist.

And the Visions Keep on Coming!
An Apocalyptic Ram, Goat, and Little Horn

DANIEL 8:1-27

Main Idea: Even in the face of impending trials, God's people receive comfort from the truth that our God is sovereign over all the nations and the leaders who rule them.

I. God Gave Daniel a Vision (8:1-14).
   A. God, who knows the future, predicted the rise of Medo-Persia (8:1-4).
   B. God, who knows the future, predicted the rise of Greece and Alexander the Great (8:5-8).
   C. God, who knows the future, predicted the rise of Antiochus IV Epiphanes (8:9-14).

II. God Sent Gabriel with an Interpretation (8:15-27).
   A. Understanding God's Word requires divine assistance (8:15-17).
   B. Understanding God's Word prepares us for what is coming (8:18-26).
   C. Understanding God's Word can be personally overpowering (8:27).

I am a huge fan of expository preaching for many reasons. Because I believe the Bible, all of it, to be inspired, inerrant, and infallible, I feel a spiritual obligation to honor the text as it was given to us by God. This is his Word, and I must rightly handle this "word of truth" (2 Tim 2:15). I should never, ever tamper with it.

There is another reason I am committed to book-by-book, chapter-by-chapter, and verse-by-verse preaching of the Bible. It forces us to handle tough texts and tough issues—texts and issues we would gladly ignore or neglect. Daniel 8 is one of those tough texts (so is Daniel 9–12!). It is that kind of text you would only go to if you were preaching chapter by chapter through the book of Daniel. Otherwise, you would give it a pass.

Daniel 8 is where we move from the Aramaic language that began in 2:4 back to the Hebrew language, which will be used for the remainder of the book. Chapters 8–12 deal with Israel and what lies in her future.

Hebrew is more fitting because this was the language of God's people. This is also the second apocalyptic vision we encounter in Daniel 7–12, but it is not the last. It is related to both Daniel 2 and 7. It covers similar material, but it also introduces things that are new. This text orbits around three main characters: a ram, a goat, and a "little horn" (8:9). Some things in this text are clearly explained for us. Others are less clear, requiring humility and our best educated guesses. Once more we will be comforted and encouraged by the truth that our God is sovereign over all the nations and the leaders who rule them. As Daniel 2:21 affirms of our Lord, "He removes kings and establishes kings" (cf. 4:17,25,32). Tyrants of this age strut briefly on the stage. God raises them up, and he takes them out. If our God has this kind of power over the nations and its rulers, surely that same power is in control of our lives as well. That is good news when rams, goats, and little horns are running wild among the nations!

Our chapter divides easily into two major sections: (1) a vision in verses 1-14 and (2) the interpretation in verses 15-27.

God Gave Daniel a Vision
DANIEL 8:1-14

Daniel 7 and 8 are related but different. Chapter 7 gave a vision of the four great kingdoms of Babylon, Medo-Persia, Greece, and Rome. Chapter 8 provides a vision that narrows the focus to Medo-Persia and Greece. It will particularly detail personalities and events related to Greece and what will transpire during its rise to power (331–146 BC). That period will be a tumultuous and troubling time for God's people, especially toward the end. They will suffer greatly. God, in grace, is preparing them ahead of time. God's people had never before faced what they would in the little horn, a man named Antiochus Epiphanes, an evil antichrist-type ruler who would institute

> a systematic programme designed to eradicate completely every trace of Israel's faith, worship, and life. Hence the extreme emergency justified the detailed prediction. The day would come when Israel would need this revelation. (Davis, *Message of Daniel*, 112)

John Calvin says it well:

> The faithful were informed beforehand of these grievous and oppressive calamities, to induce them to look up to God

when oppressed by such extreme darkness." (Beckwith, *Ezekiel, Daniel,* 345)

I believe this is a good word for us today as well.

God, Who Knows the Future, Predicted the Rise of Medo-Persia (8:1-4)

Daniel received a second vision following the first one of chapter 7. The prior vision was in the first year of Belshazzar's reign (7:1; ca. 553 BC). This one was in his third year (ca. 550 BC), two or three years later. Note the repetition of the words "vision" and "saw" throughout the chapter. Daniel is not reading a book. He is watching a sci-fi motion picture. He is seeing and breathing in the fast-moving action.

The vision takes place "in the fortress city of Susa, in the province of Elam . . . beside the Ulai Canal" (8:2). We should not think that Daniel had physically moved 220 miles east of Babylon and 150 miles north of the Persian Gulf to what is modern-day Iran. No, like John being carried "away in the Spirit to a great, high mountain" (Rev 21:10), Daniel is transported by a vision to Susa, the capital of Elam. Interestingly, the Code of Hammurabi was discovered in Susa in 1901 (Miller, *Daniel,* 221).

Daniel "looked up, and there was a ram" with two long (ESV, "high") horns, though "one was longer than the other, and the longer one came up last" (v. 3). This is Medo-Persia (v. 20). The longer, stronger, higher horn denotes Persia's greater strength and dominance. The ram was an appropriate symbol for this empire in the vision, as the Persians themselves used the animal as they marched into battle (Miller, *Daniel,* 222). The ram, under King Cyrus and his successors, extended their empire charging "to the west, the north, and the south" (v. 4). No one could stop the ram. No one could "rescue from his power. He did whatever he wanted and became great." For quite a while, it appears indestructible and unbeatable. And it is, until God raises up and sends a male goat unlike anything the world has ever seen!

God, Who Knows the Future, Predicted the Rise of Greece and Alexander the Great (8:5-8)

The ram looked invincible until it was blitzkrieged by a male goat. Think how invincible the Carolina Panthers appeared until they got trampled by the Broncos from Denver in Super Bowl 50! Likewise, Napoleon and Hitler each rampaged for a short time before encountering their Waterloo and eastern front, respectively. The male goat comes from the west so fast he does not even touch the ground, and the whole earth feels his fury. He also has "a conspicuous horn between his eyes" (v. 5). All agree this is Greece (the male goat) and Alexander the Great (the conspicuous horn). Verse 21 makes this plain. Alexander's life would be brief (356–323 BC), just thirty-three years, but his influence in spreading Greek culture is still with us to this day, especially in the Western world.

Alexander and his Greek armies came against Persia (vv. 6-7) "with savage fury" (ESV, "powerful wrath"). He quickly and decisively defeated and destroyed the Persian Empire. The verbs in verse 7 are truly striking: "infuriated," "struck," "breaking," "threw . . . to the ground," "trampled." Indeed, "there was no one to rescue the ram from his power." The lights went out on the ram when the male goat arrived on the scene. He was vanquished to the dustbin of history. The ram is dead! Long live the goat!

Alexander and Greece do become great and powerful overnight (v. 8). However, at the pinnacle of power, Alexander dies ("the large horn was broken"). Four kings will divide up his kingdom and continue in various forms until mighty Rome comes on the scene. The detail and accuracy of God's prophetic word is truly amazing. Daniel is seeing this and writing it hundreds of years in advance.

God, Who Knows the Future, Predicted the Rise of Antiochus IV Epiphanes (8:9-14)

Alexander's kingdom, following his death, was divided among four of his generals: Cassander over Macedon and Greece, Lysimachus over Thrace and Asia Minor, Seleucus over Syria and Babylon, and Ptolemy over Egypt (vv. 8,22). In verse 9 the vision Daniel receives suddenly narrows its focus to just one of them and a little horn that "emerged and grew extensively toward the south [i.e., Egypt] and the east [i.e., Persia] and toward the beautiful land [i.e., Israel]." Students of Scripture are again unanimous that this little horn is the evil king Antiochus IV, who emerged from the Seleucid Empire many years after the death of Alexander the Great. He would reign from 175 to 163 BC and severely persecute God's people.

The accuracy with which his exploits are catalogued has caused liberal scholars to deny the authenticity of Daniel's prophetic prediction. Surely what we read here, they reason, is *vaticinium ex eventu*, "prophecy after or from the event." They say that Daniel did not write this in the sixth century; a pseudonymous author penned it under Daniel's name in the second century after these events had already occurred.

For those of us who believe in a supernatural God who knows all things past, present, and future, such a move of interpretation and understanding is totally unnecessary. It is wrong. God gave Daniel a vision to prepare his people for what was coming, not what had already happened! The latter would not provide much help.

The horrible deeds of Antiochus IV Epiphanes (a title Antiochus gave himself, meaning "God Manifest" or "The Illustrious God"; his enemies called him Epimanes meaning "Madman") are addressed in verses 10-14 and 23-26. We will address them in the manner they are given in the text.

An important clarification is in order. The little horn of chapter 8 is not the little horn of 7:8. That little horn is the end-time antichrist. The little horn of chapter 8 is Antiochus IV, who does serve well as a type of the antichrist. Their attitudes and actions are similar, even parallel in how they treat God's people.

Antiochus's persecution of Israel began around 170 BC and would last right at seven years. As he grew in power and pride ("it grew as high as the heavenly army," a reference to God's people, angels, or both), he "made some of the army and some of the stars fall to the earth, and trampled them" (v. 10). He brutally persecuted God's people, which in his mind he had every right to do. Joyce Baldwin well says, "The little horn, in reaching for the stars, is claiming equality with God" (*Daniel*, 157). Verses 11-12 bear this out. He proclaims equality with God, the "Prince of the heavenly army," and his reign of terror begins. As we will see, he stops the daily worship of sacrifice and destroys the place of God's sanctuary. He "threw truth [i.e., God's Word] to the ground," counting it as worthless. For a time he "was successful" in what he did. Verses 13-14 reveal all of this will continue "for 2,300 evenings and mornings; then the sanctuary will be restored." The 2,300 evenings and mornings may mean approximately seven years, or it may refer to approximately three and a half years (roughly 1,150 days). In 168 BC the temple was desecrated. In 164 BC it was cleansed and restored. That fits well with the three and a half years understanding.

All of this is exactly what happened. We will provide a historical summary of the key events toward the end of our study. For now, suffice it to say our God knows the future, and in grace he lets his people in on many of the details to prepare them for what is coming.

God Sent Gabriel with an Interpretation
DANIEL 8:15-27

God's revelation of himself in the Bible is a gift. God's interpretation of his revelation is a double gift. Without God's revelation in Scripture we might draw conclusions from general revelation (nature and conscience) that a supreme being exists, that the supreme being is powerful, and that the supreme being is moral in some way (Ps 19; Rom 1–2). Beyond that, we would be left in the dark. Thankfully, the Christian God is a talking God who delights in revealing himself to his people. In Daniel 8:15-27, God sends his angel Gabriel to help his prophet Daniel to get a hold on the vision of 8:1-14.

This much Daniel already knows: a little horn of great depravity will arise and make himself great, even claiming divine status for himself (v. 11). He will defeat the saints (v. 10), defile the sanctuary (the temple and holy place; vv. 11,13), and disregard the Scriptures (v. 12). He will do so for twenty-three hundred evenings and mornings, a period of six to seven years or, more likely, three to four years (again depending on how one interprets the phrase).

This is a lot to consider, but specifics are still wanting. Though under no obligation, God, in grace, helps Daniel in "trying to understand it" (v. 15).

Understanding God's Word Requires Divine Assistance (8:15-17)

Daniel is "watching the vision and trying to understand it" (v. 15). Suddenly, he says, "there stood before me someone who appeared to be a man." His name is Gabriel; he's an angel of God (v. 16). His name means "Strong Man of God," or possibly "God Is My Hero/Warrior." Andrew Hill points out,

> Only in Daniel in the Old Testament are angels named
> (Gabriel in 8:16; 9:21 [cf. Luke 1:19,26]; Michael in 10:13,21;
> 12 [cf. Jude 9; Rev 12:7]). ("Daniel," 152)

God has sent him to "explain the vision" to Daniel. Without divine aid, Daniel would not be able to comprehend what he saw.

Not surprisingly, Daniel is terrified as Gabriel approaches him (v. 17). He "fell facedown" prostrate before the heavenly messenger. Gabriel addresses Daniel as "son of man" (or "son of Adam"), in this context meaning a mere human, one who is mortal. It is not a

Christological title, as it is in 7:13. Gabriel tells Daniel he has come to help him "understand that the vision refers to the time of the end." We hear that phrase and think of the end of the age, the second coming of Christ, and the millennial kingdom. However, in context it is more likely a reference to the particular persons and events prophesied in this chapter. In particular, it likely refers to Antiochus IV and his persecution of the Jewish people. Still, as Stephen Miller notes,

> It is possible to be true to the text and allow that the little horn of chapter 8, Antiochus IV, may be a type of that one spoken of in chapter 7, the eschatological antichrist, for the parallels between their characters and careers are striking. (*Daniel*, 232)

Understanding God's Word Prepares Us for What Is Coming (8:18-26)

The angel Gabriel starts talking (v. 18), and Daniel goes into a comatose state ("I fell into a deep sleep")! Gabriel touches him and gets him on his feet. He says, "I am here to tell you what will happen at the conclusion of the time of wrath" (v. 19), that is, the time when the persecution (and God's discipline of his people) under the Syrian Antiochus IV comes to an end. Gabriel tells him, in something of a parallel phrase, that this "refers to the appointed time of the end." The time has been determined and set by the sovereign Lord of history. God's people will suffer for their sins, but their suffering will not be indefinite. God is in absolute control of all that is and all that will happen. This includes the trials and tribulations of his people. Human powers are merely instruments in the hands of an all-powerful and providential God.

Verses 20-22 enlighten our understanding of the main characters in the vision of verses 1-15. The two-horned ram refers to Media and Persia. The shaggy goat refers to Greece. The large horn between the eyes of the goat refers to the first king (Alexander the Great). The four horns that replaced the broken horn refer to the four kingdoms (belonging to the four generals Cassander, Lysimachus, Selucus, and Ptolemy). Gabriel says, "They will rise from that nation" (Greece and Alexander), "but without its power." They will be mini-empires, not major ones on the scale of Medo-Persia and Greece.

Verses 23-26 then turn to Antiochus Epiphanes, referred to as "a ruthless king, skilled in intrigue" (v. 23). The English Standard Version calls him "a king of bold face." He is characterized by arrogance and pride. He will arise "near the end of their kingdoms" (175–163 BC) because mighty Rome is on the way. This will happen "when the rebels [i.e., God's rebellious people] have reached the full measure of their sin." Verse 12 provides helpful commentary on this understanding. God is once more disciplining his people for their sin.

The words "he" and "his" are prominent in verses 24-25, enabling us to outline the activities of the "ruthless king" who "will come to the throne" (v. 23).

- "His power will be great, but it will not be his own" (v. 24). He is a satanically empowered puppet.
- "He will cause outrageous destruction and succeed in whatever he does" (v. 24; cf. v. 12). He will be victorious in battle, achieve power, and amass wealth.
- "He will destroy the powerful along with the holy people" (v. 24). He will defeat many opponents in war and will war successfully against God's people for right at seven years.
- "He will cause deceit to prosper through his cunning and by his influence" (v. 25). Antiochus Epiphanes will be shrewd and deceptive, stopping at nothing to further his agenda and prosper his hand. Double-faced agreements and duplicitous dealings are his calling cards.
- He will "in his own mind . . . exalt himself" (v. 25; cf. v. 11). Arrogance, pride, and self-deification are his unholy trinity.
- "He will destroy many in a time of peace" (v. 25). He is a ruthless and unconscionable murderer.
- "He will even stand against the Prince of princes" (v. 25). He stands in opposition to God himself because he thinks he is a god (Zeus manifest).
- "Yet he will be broken—not by human hands" (v. 25). His reign will be short and his downfall devastating, all at the hands of the God he mocks and opposes.

Despite the gravity and grotesqueness of this image, Gabriel affirms the vision is true (v. 26). Daniel must write it down, seal it up, and preserve it for those in days yet to come who will need it. Remember, what is in the past to us was in the future to Daniel. He must safeguard it for future generations.

So, did the Bible get it right in Daniel 8? The answer is a resounding yes! A brief historical summary adds a little meat to the bones of Daniel's prophecy. Antiochus Epiphanes was violently bitter against the Jews. He hated them and was determined to exterminate them and their religion. He devastated Jerusalem in 168 BC, murdered tens of thousands, defiled the temple, offered a pig on its altar, erected a shrine to Jupiter, prohibited temple worship, forbade circumcision on pain of death, sold (according to 2 Macc 5:11-14) forty thousand Jews into slavery, destroyed all copies of Scripture that could be found, and slaughtered everyone found to be in possession of God's Torah. He resorted to every conceivable torture to force Jews to renounce their religion.

This all eventually led to what historians call the Maccabean revolt in 164 BC. Judas Maccabees (meaning "the hammer") would lead the Jews to victory and the restoration of their religion. Today Jews celebrate Hanukkah (the Festival of Lights) in remembrance of that event. It is referenced in John 10:22, when the Light of the World walked into the temple.

And Antiochus? The Jewish book of 2 Maccabees records his end:

> But the all-seeing Lord, the God of Israel, struck him an
> incurable and unseen blow. As soon as he ceased speaking he
> was seized with a pain in his bowels for which there was no
> relief and with sharp internal tortures—and that very justly, for
> he had tortured the bowels of others with many and strange
> inflictions. Yet he did not in any way stop his insolence, but
> was even more filled with arrogance, breathing fire in his rage
> against the Jews, and giving orders to hasten the journey. And
> so it came about that he fell out of his chariot as it was rushing
> along, and the fall was so hard as to torture every limb of his
> body. (2 Macc 9:5-7)

And just like that, the evil and ruthless king was gone.

Understanding God's Word Can Be Personally Overpowering (8:27)

What Daniel saw and took in wiped him out. It was personally overpowering. He was "overcome and lay sick for days." The New International Version says, "I was worn out. I lay exhausted for several days." *The Message* paraphrase says, "I . . . walked around in a daze, unwell for days." Daniel had been "deeply distressed," even "terrified" by the vision of chapter 7. He is completely undone by the vision of chapter 8. It was more than he could bear. He was comforted by the reality that God was in control and that his kingdom would eventually come (v. 25b), but to know that there would be so much evil in the world and so much suffering for God's people before it arrived was overwhelming. It was too much, at least for a while.

Daniel's sickness passed. God's grace was sufficient. Regaining his strength, God's prophet got up and went back to work as he normally would: "I got up and went about the king's business" (v. 27). Sinclair Ferguson says it well:

> He returned to the duties to which God had called him. He did not retire from the world in view of the evil days that were coming. Nor did he go to the opposite extreme and live on a "high" visionary excitement. Instead he did his duty.
>
> Daniel's attitude illustrates an important biblical principle: In view of what the future holds, we must live holy lives now. He caught a glimpse of realities that would take place centuries later. Those events were shadows of the last conflict between the kingdom of Christ and the kingdoms of the world. One day Christ will return and the Antichrist "shall be broken without human hands" just as Antiochus was. We know this from the New Testament. How then should we live? Passage after passage gives the same answer: Do the King's business; walk in obedience; live in holiness; purify yourself as He is pure. While riding to a preaching engagement one day, John Wesley was stopped by a stranger who asked him what he would do if he knew that Christ was going to return at noon the next day. Wesley reached into his saddlebag, retrieved his diary, read out his engagements for the rest of the day and for the morning of the next day, and said, "That, dear sir, is what I would do." His knowledge of the Lord's future kingdom allowed him to live already for that kingdom. That was the spirit of Daniel. Is it so surprising that his life made such a lasting impression? (*Daniel,* 165)

The vision "greatly disturbed" him and he "could not understand it." Nevertheless, Daniel did not let it paralyze him. He did his job, and he trusted in his God. He is an example to all of us.

Conclusion: How Does This Text Point to Christ?

Daniel 8 should be read in the light of Daniel 7, which speaks of Christ as the coming Son of Man, and Daniel 9, which speaks of Christ as "the Anointed One [who] will be cut off" (9:26). Doing so sheds light on the identity of "the Prince of the heavenly army" in 8:11 and "the Prince of princes" in 8:25. All four titles point to Christ, the One who will shatter the "ruthless king" (v. 23) but "not by human hands" (v. 25). Parallels with the Prince of Daniel 8 and the Messiah Prince in the New Testament are helpfully highlighted by Sidney Greidanus:

> The first major analogy is that both were attacked by evil people. "The Prince of the host" was attacked by the evil king (8:11,25). Jesus was also attacked but much more severely. When Jesus was born, King Herod tried to kill him (Matt 2:13); the devil tempted him three times (Matt 4:1-10); the people of his hometown of Nazareth tried to "hurl him off the cliff" (Luke 4:28); "The chief priests and the scribes were looking for a way to put Jesus to death" (Luke 22:2); Pilate had Jesus flogged and then "handed him over to be crucified" (Matt 27:26); the Roman soldiers mocked Jesus, "spat on him," struck him on the head with a reed, and crucified him (Matt 27:30-35). Surely, the spirit of the Antichrist was at work attacking the Christ even during Jesus' own lifetime.
>
> The second major analogy is that the attacker will be destroyed. Daniel 8:25 declares that the evil king "shall even rise up against the Prince of princes. But he shall be broken, and not by human hands." The implication is that "the Prince of princes" will break the evil king. This prediction was fulfilled when King Antiochus was destroyed. But it will find final fulfillment at Jesus' Second Coming. Paul writes about the end of time: "Then the lawless one [the antichrist] will be revealed, whom the Lord Jesus will destroy with the breath of his mouth, annihilating him by the manifestation of his coming" (2 Thess 2:8). (*Preaching Christ from Daniel*, 268)

To this helpful insight, David Helm rightly adds,

> In his earthly ministry, Jesus entered the temple at a time of religious degradation and laid claim on restoring it to its rightful place (John 2:13-22) [contra Antiochus and his evil

actions]. . . . Jesus' substitutionary death and resurrection put
an end to the need for morning and evening sacrifices once
and for all (Hebrews 10:1-18). . . . The final word is not had by
the ram, or the goat, but by the Lamb. (*Daniel for You,* 154–55)

Reflect and Discuss

1. How does Daniel's vision point to the graciousness of all divine
   revelation?
2. An emphasis of this chapter is that God knows the future. What
   effects should this truth have on your daily life?
3. Why do you think it was necessary and helpful for God to reveal the
   coming kingdoms to the people of Israel?
4. What do these verses reveal about each of the kingdoms represented? What characterizes each of them?
5. If God had not revealed himself in Scripture, what could we know
   about him? How do you know?
6. What divine assistance is there for the Christian as he or she reads
   and interprets Scripture?
7. How does Daniel's vision show both God's judgment of evil nations
   and his discipline of his people?
8. Have you ever been overpowered or overwhelmed by the truths of
   Scripture, as Daniel was in this text? What were you reading, and
   why was it so powerful?
9. Why is it wrong to be complacent in this life, knowing that ultimate
   victory belongs to Christ?
10. How does Antiochus IV Epiphanes contrast in both his work and his
    character with the coming Messiah, Jesus Christ?

Lessons on Prayer from a Man of God

DANIEL 9:1-19

Main Idea: God's people are marked by humble confession and great confidence in the righteousness and faithfulness of God.

I. Let Your Prayers Flow from Your Study of the Scriptures (9:1-2).
II. Let Your Prayers Humbly Take You into the Presence of God (9:3).
III. Let Your Prayers Be Characterized by Honest and Full Confession of Sin (9:4-14).
IV. Let Your Prayers Move to Petition and Pleas Grounded in God's Character (9:15-19).

The wonderful seventeenth-century Puritan, John Owen, well said, "What an individual is in secret, on his knees before God, that he is and no more" (Ferguson, *Daniel,* 171). If Owen is right, and I believe he is, then Daniel was quite a man. This is certainly what God thought. In Daniel 9:23, the angel Gabriel says of the prophet, "You are treasured by God." The English Standard Version translates it, "You are greatly loved." The New International Version says, "You are highly esteemed."

Daniel 9:1-19 contains one of the most remarkable prayers in the whole Bible. It runs on the dual tracks of (1) corporate confession of sin and (2) recognition of the greatness, awesomeness, righteousness, and holiness of God as expressions of his character. It is a model prayer for how God's people should pray for a nation. But even more, it is a model for how God's people should pray for a desolate and rebellious community of faith. This passage shows God's man confessing and interceding for God's sinful people!

The brokenness and humility of Daniel as he prays for "all Israel" (v. 7) is amazing. Yet we should not be surprised. As the faithful Baptist preacher of London, Charles Spurgeon, said,

> A True-Hearted believer does not live for himself. Where there is abundance of grace, a great strength of mind in the service of God, there is sure to be a spirit of unselfishness. . . .

Daniel's prayer should, by the blessing of God's Spirit, inspire us with the spirit of prayer; and that his example, in forgetting himself, and remembering his people, should help us to be unselfish, and lead us to care for our people—even God's people—to whom we have the honor and privilege to belong. (*Sermons on the Book of Daniel*, 99–100)

We are going to look at this prayer in four movements: verses 1-2, 3, 4-14, and 15-19. And we will bracket each movement with great statements on prayer from precious saints who have delighted in talking to our heavenly Father. In doing so, we will immerse ourselves in the purifying waters of prayer, asking God to make us men and women of prayer like we see exemplified in his prophet named Daniel.

Let Your Prayers Flow from Your Study of the Scriptures
DANIEL 9:1-2

Don't pray when you feel like it. Have an appointment with the Lord and keep it.

Corrie ten Boom

Daniel provides a historical marker for us in verse 1: it was the first year of Darius the Mede (another name or title for Cyrus; cf. 5:31; 6:1). The date is ca. 538 BC, approximately twelve years after the vision recorded in chapter 8 (Miller, *Daniel*, 240). Daniel is now more than eighty years old. He outlived the Babylonian Empire and now serves under Medo-Persia.

Daniel is reading the Bible, "the books according to the word of the LORD" (v. 2). Specifically, he is reading in the prophet Jeremiah "that the number of years for the desolation of Jerusalem would be seventy." This predictive promise is found in Jeremiah 25:1-14 and 29:1-11. We must not miss the important point that Daniel considered Jeremiah to be Scripture in calling it "the books" or literally "the writings" (Hb *sepharim*). The Hebrew canon was not complete, but Jeremiah was already a part of sacred Scripture.

God judged Israel as he promised he would in Deuteronomy 28:15-68. Jeremiah reveals this exile would last seventy years. Daniel was exiled with others in 605 BC (cf. Dan 1:1-4). It is now 538 BC, and Daniel, in reading Jeremiah, knows the end of God's judgment of exile on his people is coming. And he knows that Yahweh ("the LORD" in 9:2,4) is a covenant God who keeps his word (cf. Ezra 1:1). Further, as Bob Fyall succinctly says, "What Scripture says is what God says, and what God says happens" (*Daniel*, 132).

When God makes a promise in his Word, it is not conditional or potential. It will come to pass just as he says it will. No other god can do that because all other gods are mere idols, often empowered and energized by demons. Isaiah 44:6-20 contains a scathing denouncement on them and those who make and worship them.

Daniel believed in predictive prophecy, as should we. He saw it as he read and meditated on Scripture and trusted it as a reliable word from God. Exiled, captive in a godless land, and moving rapidly toward the end of his life, he still had great hope for his people in light of the sure and certain promises of the Word of God. Confidence in the promises of God did not move him to complacency. It drove him to action and to his knees. Immersion in Scripture will energize prayer!

So reflecting on these two verses, we would all do well to ask, Do I struggle to pray as I ought because I do not know Scripture as I should? Do I fail to approach my God well because I do not soak in his Word well? God delights in the prayers of his children that emerge out of time in his Word.

> Only as we deepen our understanding of God as revealed in the Bible will our praying become richer and more soundly based on who God is. (Fyall, *Daniel*, 147)

Let Your Prayers Humbly Take You into the Presence of God
DANIEL 9:3

> Where the mind isn't brimming with the Bible, the heart is not generally brimming with prayer.
> John Piper, "How to Pray for a Desolate Church," 1992

Verse 3 describes the humble and contrite attitude with which Daniel approached "the Lord God" in prayer. He began by turning from his reading of the Scriptures to seek the face of "the LORD my God" (v. 4). René Péter-Contesse and John Ellington note that in the context of Bible translation, "a literal rendering of the verb phrase **turned my face** will probably sound strange in many languages. It simply focuses on the beginning of the action of earnestly praying to God" (*Handbook on the Book of Daniel*, 231). A deep earnestness in Daniel's heart moves him to look to his Lord. Seeking the Lord "by prayer and pleas for mercy" (ESV), he approaches him in the threefold posture of "fasting, sackcloth, and ashes." David Helm provides a nice explanation when he writes,

> Fasting is the withholding of food from the body for the sake of prioritizing something else, such as prayer. Sackcloth was a rough material, most likely made from animal skins that would have been an irritant to the skin, and was a mark of repentance. Ashes symbolized complete ruin. In other words, the posture Daniel took was of visible lament. (*Daniel for You*, 159)

Daniel turned to the Lord with a heavy heart, a burden he could hardly bear. Indeed he could not bear it without God's help and strength. Daniel's prayer should remind us of a prayer offered in a garden called Gethsemane some six hundred years later. In Gethsemane, in prayers and petitions, our Lord Jesus turned his face to his Father in humble pleas for mercy (Luke 22:39-44). The burden of bearing the sins of the world (John 1:29) caused "his sweat [to become] like drops of blood falling to the ground" (Luke 22:44). Coming humbly, dependently, into the presence of his Father, his prayer was heard ("not my will, but yours, be done," v. 42), and strength was provided for enduring the cross that lay ahead.

Daniel humbled himself to pray. Jesus humbled himself both to pray and to prepare for his passion. It is truly unconscionable that we would ever think to burst into God's presence in arrogance or pride, in hubris or vainglory. When we know our sins and the sins of our people, we will approach God on our knees and with our faces to the ground. Only then can we turn our faces to the Lord with our prayers and pleas. Only then can we rightly pour out our hearts and souls to "the LORD [our] God."

> All vital prayer makes a drain on a man's vitality. True intercession is a sacrifice, a bleeding sacrifice.
>
> J. H. Jowett, *The Passion for Souls*, 1905

Let Your Prayers Be Characterized by Honest and Full Confession of Sin
DANIEL 9:4-14

The great people of the earth today are people who pray,
(not) those who talk about prayer.
                          S. D. Gordon, *Quiet Talks on Prayer*, 1904

The prayer of Daniel is recorded in verses 4-19. It is characterized by two major themes: (1) corporate confession of sin and (2) acknowledgement of God's character and mighty acts of salvation. John Piper notes,

> Daniel's prayer begins with the Bible and it is saturated with
> the Bible. Phrase after phrase comes right out of Scripture.
> There are allusions to Leviticus (26:40) and Deuteronomy
> (28:64) and Exodus (34:6) and Psalms (44:14) and Jeremiah
> (25:11). The prayer brims with a biblical view of reality,
> because it brims with the Bible. ("How to Pray for a Desolate
> Church")

The prayer itself can be analyzed in a number of ways, including by its structure and its content. Structurally there are three movements:

- Adoration (v. 4)
- Confession (vv. 5-14)
- Petition (vv. 15-19) (Miller, *Daniel*, 243–49)

In terms of content, one is overwhelmed by the use of the word "we" and the piling up of terms used to describe Israel and Judah's sin. Concerning the use of "we" and Daniel's solidarity with the Hebrews in their sin, Bryan Chapell well says,

> Daniel confesses the reality of his sin and the people's sin
> because he has been called to carry their burden as his
> own even though he did not cause the burden. He feels
> responsible for the people under his care. (*Gospel According to
> Daniel*, 158)

As to the terms used to describe Israel and Judah's sin, note the following: "sinned, done wrong, acted wickedly, rebelled, and turned away" (v. 5), "not listened" (v. 6), "disloyalty" (v. 7), "public shame," "sinned"

(v. 8), "rebelled" (v. 9), "not obeyed" (v. 10), "broken your law," "turned away," "refusing to obey," "sinned" (v. 11), "iniquities" (v. 13), "not obeyed" (v. 14), "sinned," "acted wickedly" (v. 15). Daniel has taken the role of prosecuting attorney and has built an irrefutable case against those who "bear [God's] name" (vv. 18-19). And amazingly, Daniel puts himself on the side of God's rebellious people by using the personal pronouns "we" or "us" or "our" more than twenty times! In a confession of sin that echoes Isaiah 6, in a confession of sin that acknowledges that they have broken their marriage covenant to Yahweh (Ezek 16:8), in a confession of sin that admits to not keeping the Lord's commands and ordinances (9:5), in a confession of sin that acknowledges they have not listened to God's prophets (v. 6)—Daniel acknowledges that his nation's exile is just and right. Why? Because "the Lord our God is righteous in all he has done" (v. 14; cf. v. 7). Israel's "public shame" (vv. 7-8) is deserved. They have disrespected "the great and awe-inspiring God who keeps his gracious covenant" (v. 4). Therefore, the promised curses written in the Law of Moses (Lev 26; Deut 28) have "been poured out on" them (v. 11). Shame on God's people and shame on God's city (v. 12) is the righteous reward they have invited on themselves.

Amazingly, this portion of the prayer (vv. 4-14) ends with the indictment, "But we have not obeyed [the Lord]." Dale Davis provides words of wisdom when he writes,

> Daniel seems to be saying that though Israel had gone
> through the ravages of God's curse, the people remained
> unchanged, unbroken, unrepentant. . . . Israel has a history
> of rebellion and idolatry and has suffered God's judgment
> for it but it has not driven them to godly grief and genuine
> repentance. . . . What good will it do to have a people back
> in the land with still no sense of their sin and no exercise in
> repentance? Who have never been crushed in spirit over their
> idolatry? It's not Israel alone—humanity in general is averse to
> admitting sin and guilt. (*Message of Daniel*, 118)

To such an accusation, we all must confess: guilty as charged.

> To get nations back on their feet, we must first get down on
> our knees.
>
>   Billy Graham

Let Your Prayers Move to Petition and Pleas Grounded in God's Character
DANIEL 9:15-19

Prayer is not so much an act as it is an attitude—an attitude of dependency, dependency upon God.

Arthur Pink, *The Sovereignty of God*, 1918

Before the righteous Judge (God) and the prosecuting attorney (Daniel), God's people have been tried and found guilty. There will be no appeal. No retrial. The evidence is too great. Actually, it is irrefutable. Is there then any hope? Is there any court or avenue of grace and forgiveness? Mercifully the answer is yes, there is! Sinclair Ferguson is so helpful here when he says,

> Daniel sees the righteousness of God both as the basis for
> God's judgment of the people (v. 7) and also the basis for
> his own prayer for forgiveness (v. 16). How can this be?
> In Scripture, "righteousness" basically means "integrity."
> Sometimes it is defined as "conformity to a norm." In the case
> of God the norm to which He conforms is His own being and
> character. He is true to Himself; He always acts in character.
> (*Daniel*, 178)

So in a prayer that is clearly God centered but people oriented (ibid., 179), Daniel appeals to "the great and awe-inspiring God who keeps his gracious covenant" (v. 4) to act for the sake of his own name, to move according to his character, righteousness, and "abundant compassion" (v. 18). In verse 15 Daniel appeals to the exodus and God's gracious deliverance of a sinful and undeserving people (then and now). In verse 16 he appeals to God's righteous acts and pleads that the Lord would turn away his "anger and wrath" from "your city Jerusalem." Why? Because "Jerusalem and your people have become an object of ridicule [ESV, "byword"] to all those around us" (cf. Hezekiah's prayer in 2 Kgs 19:14-19). Dale Davis again is right: "Daniel batters heaven with appeals to God's honor" (*Message of Daniel*, 120). It is God's city, his holy hill, his people (v. 16), his servant, his desolate sanctuary (v. 17), his name (v. 18), his own sake, his city, his people, his name (v. 19).

Daniel's plea begins to build as he asks God to "hear the prayer and the petitions of your servant. Make your face shine" (v. 17). "Listen closely, my God, and hear. Open your eyes and see" our devastation on what "bears your name." Lord, we appeal to "your abundant compassion" (v. 18). Then reaching a crescendo he cries out in verse 19: Lord, hear! Forgive! Listen and act. Do not delay. Do it not for our sake, for we are undeserving. Lord, do it for your own sake! Do it because it will bring glory to your name and show the nations just who you are and what you are like. You ruined your own reputation to drive us to repentance. Restore your name and reputation for your sake. We are not worthy. But Lord, you are!

> God shapes the world by prayer. The more praying there is in
> the world the better the world will be, the mightier the forces
> against evil.
>   E. M. Bounds, *Purpose in Prayer*, 19th c.

Conclusion: How Does This Text Point to Christ?

Alfred Tennyson says, "More things are wrought by prayer than this world dreams of" (Fyall, *Daniel: A Tale of Two Cities*, 131). The Bible teaches us how true that is, especially when a man of God intercedes for the people of God. Moses, in Exodus 32 (cf. Deut 9:13-14), pleads with God not to destroy the people for their idolatry. Instead, he asks God to take his life in their place. God did not wipe them out. Here Daniel identifies himself with his people in their sin, making their sin his sin. Both anticipate the greater Moses (Deut 18:15-20) and the greater Daniel who will identify himself with those he will save and substitute himself in death, taking their place and bearing the punishment of their sin. And we should note the important role prayer played in the past but also in the present. In the past, in the garden of Gethsemane, our Lord was troubled and wept in prayer as he prepared to take on the sins of the world and to bear in his own body the judgment and wrath of God. But now, as Romans 8:34 and Hebrews 7:25 tell us, we have an intercessor in heaven, a great high priest, who pleads our cause before "the great and awe-inspiring God who keeps his gracious covenant with those who love him and keep his commands" (Dan 9:4).

The prayer of Moses draws my admiration. The prayer of Daniel inspires my emulation. The prayers of Jesus move me to adoration. His prayers led him to experience "public shame" (v. 7) in my place. His prayers my God heard. His prayers led my God to forgive. Hearing the prayers of his own dear Son, my God paid attention and he acted, raising Jesus from the dead after which Christ ascended on high and is "able to save completely those who come to God through him, since he always lives to intercede for them" (Heb 7:25). I love praying men. I worship my praying God!

Reflect and Discuss

1. Prayer reveals much about who we truly are. What does your prayer life reveal about you?
2. What are some ways the Scriptures can and should shape our prayers?
3. What are some practical ways you can incorporate the Scriptures into your prayer life?
4. Many Christians find that it is more difficult to pray when they do not spend time in God's Word. Why do you think that is? Do you find it to be true in your own life? If so, explain.
5. Why are pride and prayer so opposed to one another?
6. Daniel brings his heavy heart to the Lord in this text. Are there any burdens you need to take to God in humility and confidence in his character?
7. What barriers or excuses do you use to avoid honest and full confession of sin to God?
8. Daniel explicitly lumps himself in with the rebellious people of Israel. How does this instruct how we should relate to other Christians?
9. How is God's discipline of his people consistent with his character? How are his mercy and forgiveness consistent with his character?
10. How does Daniel's identification with the people of Israel point to the gospel and what Christ has done for you?

Daniel's Seventy Weeks and the Glorious Work of Messiah Jesus

DANIEL 9:20-27

Main Idea: God has a plan to bring about the salvation of his people and the judgment of his enemies, and it centers on the person and work of Jesus Christ.

I. **God Hears the Passionate Prayers of His Beloved Children (9:20-23).**
   - A. Daniel prayed to God (9:20-21).
   - B. God answered Daniel's prayer (9:21-23).
II. **God Has a Prophetic Plan to Bring about Our Salvation (9:24-27).**
   - A. In his time God deals with sin (9:24).
   - B. In his time God sends Messiah Jesus (9:25-26).
   - C. In his time God judges his people (9:26).
   - D. In his time God destroys his enemies (9:27).

The great expositor Alistair Begg playfully but wisely says of Daniel 9:24-27,

> In what follows, I reserve the right to change my mind later this evening, and as often as necessary for the rest of my life, until I finally settle the matter. What I'm about to now unfold for you will annoy some, disappoint others, confuse many, and perhaps encourage a few. ("Gabriel and the 70 Weeks")

After spending dozens and dozens of hours studying this text, I fully understand his position. Joyce Baldwin says, "The last four verses [of Daniel 9] present the most difficult text in the book" (*Daniel*, 163). Stephen Miller says Daniel 9:24-27 "are four of the most controversial verses in the Bible" (*Daniel*, 252). J. A. Montgomery is perhaps the most colorful when he writes, "The history of the exegesis of the 70 weeks of Daniel is the Dismal Swamp of Old Testament criticism" ("Daniel," 168).

There is, without question, difficulty in the details. However, we must not let that reality distract us from the big picture that is clear and

117

plain for all to see. With his wonderful gift of words, Charles Spurgeon lays out God's divine plan for us:

> The Lord God appointed a set time for the coming of his Son into the world; nothing was left to chance. Infinite wisdom dictated the hour at which the Messiah should be born, and the moment at which he should be cut off. His advent and his work are the highest point of the purpose of God, the hinge of history, the centre of providence, the crowning of the edifice of grace, and therefore peculiar care watched over every detail. Once in the end of the world hath the Son of God appeared to put away sin by the sacrifice of himself, and this is the event before which all other events must bow. The studious mind will be delighted to search out the reasons why the Messiah came not before, and why he did not tarry till yet later ages. Prophecies declared the date; but long before infallible wisdom had settled it for profoundest reasons. It was well that the Redeemer came: it was well that he came in what Scripture calls the fullness of time, even in these last days.
>
> Note again, that the Lord told his people somewhat darkly, but still with a fair measure of clearness, when the Christ would come. (*Sermons on the Book of Daniel*, 121)

So God has a specific plan in which Messiah will come and deal decisively with sin, though he will be executed in the process, and many troubles will precede and follow that coming. Israel, in particular, will suffer, but God has decreed how and when the end will come. Regardless of where we are or what we are experiencing, we can trust him. He is in control. His plan will come to pass just as he has planned.

Daniel is praying for his people Israel (9:4-19). His prayer is one of deep repentance and heartfelt confession. Deuteronomy 4 and 28 said that Israel would sin, be scattered from their land, seek God (which Daniel is doing on their behalf), and return to the Lord (see Deut 4:25-31). Jeremiah 25:1-14 and 29:10-14 tell us that this particular exile in Babylon would last seventy years. Daniel understood these verses literally and recognized the exile was coming to an end. Interestingly, when King Solomon voiced his prayer of dedication for the temple in 1 Kings 8:22-53, he said that if and when Israel was sent into exile for her sin, she should seek God in prayer and repentance and he would forgive and rescue her. Daniel is doing exactly what Solomon suggested in that prayer almost five hundred years earlier.

Our passage can be divided into two parts: (1) Daniel's prayers (9:20-23), and (2) God's prophecy (9:24-27). Prepare yourself for a hermeneutical roller coaster!

God Hears the Passionate Prayers of His Beloved Children
DANIEL 9:20-23

James 4:3 has a stern warning when it comes to prayer. There the half brother of Jesus says, "You ask and don't receive because you ask with wrong motives, so that you may spend it on your pleasures" (ESV, "passions"; KJV, "lusts"). Who we pray to, what we pray for, and how we pray are all important to God. The prophet Daniel provides a marvelous example of a man whose prayer life met all the criteria to receive an answer from God.

Daniel Prayed to God (9:20-21)

Daniel 9:20-27 follows the lengthy prayer of 9:1-19. I believe this passage describes that prayer and indicates that Daniel was still praying! He is still

> speaking, praying, confessing my sin and the sin of my people
> Israel, and presenting my petition before the Lord my God concerning
> the holy mountain of my God. (v. 20)

He is praying to the right person with the right posture, something that always characterizes real and authentic praying.

While he is praying, the angel Gabriel suddenly appears in the form of a man. Daniel notes it is the same angel he had seen in his first vision (8:15-17). Gabriel means "Strong Man of God," which is appropriate because he comes to lend support to Daniel in his state of "extreme weariness" (9:21). Gabriel is mentioned twice in Daniel in chapters 8–9. In the Gospel of Luke, he appears to Zechariah and Mary announcing the births of John the Baptist and Jesus (Luke 1:11-38). Some believe he is an archangel, though the Bible never calls him one.

Daniel says the angel came "about the time of the evening offering" (Dan 9:21). That's interesting. There had been no evening sacrifices at the temple in Jerusalem since it was destroyed in 586 BC. Nevertheless, Daniel still tells time according to his religious calendar. "He still functions on 'Jerusalem time,'" says Dale Davis (*Message of Daniel,* 124). Daniel at eighty-plus years of age has not lost his spiritual identity. *Yahweh's* clock is his clock.

God Answered Daniel's Prayer (9:21-23)

God sent his angel Gabriel while Daniel was praying (v. 21). He is there to help Daniel understand, "to give [him] understanding" (v. 22). While some make a connection here to the vision of chapter 8, I believe it is better to see Gabriel answering Daniel's prayer in chapter 9 and providing an explanation of Israel's exile and her future—things that were the concerns of Daniel's prayer.

In verse 23 Gabriel tells Daniel that the moment he began praying "an answer went out, and I have come to give it." Why? The text tells us clearly: "For you are treasured by God." Those whom the Lord greatly loves, he hears. Those who are greatly loved, our God honors. Daniel is precious in the sight of God, and therefore so are his prayers. God values the prayers of his faithful and righteous saints. He treasures them. Gabriel has been sent directly by God with an answer to Daniel's prayer. Therefore, Daniel should carefully "consider the message and understand the vision" through the appearance and words of Gabriel. Daniel is about to receive one of the greatest and most important visions and revelations in the whole Bible. His alertness and readiness is a must.

God Has a Prophetic Plan to Bring about Our Salvation
DANIEL 9:24-27

Verses 24-27 address the "seventy weeks" (or better, the "seventy sevens") prophecy of Daniel. Virtually all scholars agree that the "sevens" represent years rather than weeks. The word "seven" functions like our English word "dozen." It can refer to seven days, weeks, months, or years. God is telling Daniel that Israel's exile will not last seventy years. It will last seventy times seven years, or four hundred ninety years. The Hebrews would have readily understood this ambiguity between days and years. Not only did they celebrate the Sabbath every seven days, but they were also supposed to celebrate a "Sabbath year" every seven years according to Leviticus 25:1-7. Unfortunately, they had disobeyed the command, and that was one of the reasons they were exiled for seventy years (cf. Lev 26:33-35; 2 Chron 36:21).

Four major views are held by various scholars today on how to understand the seventy sevens. I will quickly note them and then move into our verses defending the view I think is the best understanding at the time I am writing this.[5]

View 1. The seventy sevens are literal years that run from either 605 or 586 BC to the reign of Antiochus (Epiphanes) in 167–164 BC. The dates, however, simply do not work, and this view does not fit well with what Daniel 9:24-27 actually says. This is a view usually advocated by more liberal scholars.

View 2. The seventy sevens are symbolic periods of time culminating in the first century AD. This view also struggles with dates and the content of the prophecy.

View 3. The seventy sevens are symbolic periods of time ending with the second coming of Christ.

> The seventy 7's are a prophecy of church history (both the
> Old Testament and the New Testament church) from Cyrus'
> decree in 538 BC until the return of Christ at the end of the
> age. (Miller, *Daniel,* 255)

I find this view unconvincing as well.

View 4. The seventy sevens are literal years that end with Christ's second coming but also include his first coming. And there is an important prophetic gap between the sixty-ninth and seventieth week. The first sixty-nine weeks are now past. The climactic seventieth week is still future. Stephen Miller lays this scenario out, and his view is the one I find the most convincing overall.

> The first seven sevens (forty-nine years) commence with
> a command to rebuild Jerusalem (either the decree to
> Ezra in 458 B.C. or the decree to Nehemiah in 445 B.C.)
> and terminate with the completion of the work of Ezra
> and Nehemiah about forty-nine years later (either ca. 409
> B.C. or ca. 396 B.C.). The next sixty-two sevens (434 years)
> extend from the end of the first group of sevens to Christ's
> first coming (either his baptism in ca. A.D. 26 or Christ's
> presentation of himself to the people as Messiah on Palm
> Sunday in A.D. 32/33). (*Daniel,* 257)

---

[5] For this summary, I am following Stephen Miller and his fine work on Daniel: Miller, *Daniel,* 253–57.

The seventieth week is separated in time from the sixty-nine. Daniel 9:26b-27 looks both to the destruction of Jerusalem in AD 70 and the coming of the antichrist at the end of the age. Titus, the Roman general, is a forerunner and type of the antichrist. The destruction of Jerusalem in AD 70 foreshadows an end-time persecution that will exceed anything the world has ever known. I believe this is the understanding of Jesus according to his teaching in the Olivet Discourse in Matthew 24 (note especially vv. 15-28).

Let's walk through these four verses humbly and carefully. I will note what we can be more sure of. And I will again remind us that we should tread softly where angels fear to go.

In His Time God Deals with Sin (9:24)

Gabriel tells Daniel, "Seventy sevens" (the literal rendering) "are decreed about your people [Israel] and your holy city [Jerusalem]." Robert Fyall notes,

> Behind all biblical uses of seven lie the seven days of creation. Thus the return from Exile is not simply a new Exodus, but a new creation and thus foreshadows the end time. (*Daniel,* 142)

During the seventy sevens, six things will occur:

- Rebellion will be finished.
- An end to sin is to be made.
- Atonement for iniquity will take place.
- Everlasting righteousness is to be brought in.
- Vision and prophecy will be sealed up.
- The most holy place or Holy One will be anointed.

Anyone with even limited knowledge and understanding of the Bible and the Christian faith could read this and immediately respond, "This is talking about Jesus and what he did for us." During the seventy weeks, sin is dealt with once and for all by means of atonement when "an Anointed One, the ruler" is cut off, crucified after sixty-nine weeks (vv. 25-26). His atoning sacrifice is God's final word and will usher in everlasting righteousness through the anointing of the most holy place—perhaps a future temple like that described in Ezekiel 40–48, or possibly the Holy One Jesus who constitutes a new temple himself and in his body, the church (John 2:18-21; 1 Cor 3:16; Eph 2:19-21). Regardless, sin is coming to an end! The anointed ruler and his work of atonement will see to it.

In His Time God Sends Messiah Jesus (9:25-26)

Daniel 9:25-27 focuses on three events that take place during the 490 years: The *first* is the rebuilding of Jerusalem (v. 25) during the first seven weeks, or forty-nine years. The *second* is the coming and death of Messiah (v. 26) during the seven plus sixty-two weeks, or 483 years. And the *third* is the persecution by the antichrist (the coming ruler of the people) and his defeat (v. 27) in the final or seventieth week.

In verse 25 Daniel is told to know and understand that "from the going out of the word to restore and build Jerusalem to the coming of an anointed one, a prince, there shall be seven weeks" (ESV; i.e., forty-nine years).

This "going out of the word" or "issuing of the decree" is probably a reference to the decree of Artaxerxes I to Ezra in 458 BC or a second decree of Artaxerxes I to Nehemiah in 445/444 BC. Though dogmatism is unwarranted, I favor the 458 BC date as the correct beginning point for the seventy sevens. The temple, city, and walls would be rebuilt, but troubles would accompany the rebuilding every step of the way—especially during the first forty-nine years as the book of Nehemiah makes clear.

Verse 26 then informs us that after the sixty-two weeks (plus the prior seven, equaling sixty-nine weeks, or 483 years), the anointed ruler, the Messiah, "will be cut off and will have nothing." If 458 BC is correct, 483 years brings us to ca. AD 26–27—the time of Christ and the beginning of his public ministry. This is a remarkable prediction and fulfillment. What amazing accuracy!

Then, sometime after the sixty-ninth week, probably a short time, Messiah is cut off and left with nothing (9:26a). He is put to death and appears to be "cut off from the land of the living" (Isa 53:8). James Boice summarizes well our text at this point:

> By whatever set of calculations one makes, the point is that by the end of the sixty-nine weeks of years [or shortly after] the great work of the atonement of the Lord Jesus Christ for sin should be completed. (*Daniel*, 101)

In His Time God Judges His People (9:26-27)

Messiah has been rejected. Judgment follows from what Gabriel calls "the people of the coming ruler." I believe the Romans and General Titus were typical of this prophecy in the destruction of Jerusalem and the temple in AD 70. The end of Israel indeed was like a flood, and it was a tragic and horrible war. Indeed, "desolations are decreed" (9:26b). But this is not the end. There is a common prophetic gap between the sixty-ninth and seventieth week. Robert Gundry says it well:

> The possibility of gap between the sixty-ninth and the seventieth weeks is established by the well accepted Old Testament phenomenon of prophetic perspective, in which gaps such as that between the first and second advents were not perceived. (*The Church and the Tribulation,* 190)

This fits with the biblical narrative, in which Messiah is cut off at or shortly after the end of the sixty-ninth week, and Jerusalem and the temple are destroyed after the sixty-ninth week but before the seventieth week.

In His Time God Will Destroy His Enemies (9:27)

Verse 27 deals with the seventieth week, the last seven years of history prior to the coming of God's kingdom in its full and glorious manifestation. It begins when he, the ruler of verse 26, makes "a firm covenant with many for one week" (v. 27). Typified by Titus, this is the antichrist, the little horn of Daniel 7:8. He is a deceiver and persecutor of God's people. The antichrist, or the coming ruler, makes this "firm covenant" with many. This is probably a reference to the Jewish people (though some identify this group more specifically as either unbelieving Jews or even true believers). At the midpoint of the time period (three and a half years), he apparently breaks the covenant and puts an end to sacrifice and offering. Worship of the true God, or anyone other than him, is outlawed and forbidden (see Rev 13). The phrase "And the abomination of desolation will be on a wing of the temple" most likely speaks of the spreading of abominations in the context of idolatry. This will continue but not forever. It will continue "until the decreed destruction is poured out on the desolator"—until God stops it and in the process pours out his judgment and wrath on the antichrist. Stephen Miller, quoting from the NIV, handles these difficult verses as well as anyone:

> Antichrist's incredible atrocities against his fellow human beings and his attacks upon God himself (cf. 7:21-25) will include even the idolatrous claim that he is deity with an attempt at forced worship of himself (cf. 2 Thess. 2:4; Rev. 13:8,14-17).
>
> "One who causes desolation" (similar to NASB) refers to Antichrist, who will forbid worship and thereby make the

temple area desolate (empty). Rather than being an object that desolates in this context, it appears to be the Antichrist himself who desolates. This person's terrible atrocities ("abominations") and the fact he causes the temple to be desolate (because of religious persecution) results in the judgment announced in the latter part of the verse.

This will be a terrible period in the world's history, but the Lord has "decreed" that these atrocities will not continue forever. Antichrist's wickedness will last only "until the end that is decreed is poured out on him." "Poured out" picturesquely describes the flood of judgment that will overtake the Antichrist (cf. 7:9-11,26; 2 Thess. 2:8; Rev. 19:19-21). "On him" is literally "on the desolating one" ("desolator," NRSV; Heb. *šōmēn*), a reference to Antichrist, which will cause the temple to become desolate. (*Daniel*, 273)

Dale Davis succinctly adds,

A final ruler then exalts himself, imposes his authority, forbids true worship, instigates idolatrous worship and runs into the meat-grinder of God's decree. Predetermined. On target. Certain. (*The Message of Daniel*, 137–38)

Conclusion: How Does This Text Point to Christ?

Daniel sees from Jeremiah that exile will last seventy years. Therefore, he prays a prayer of repentance and confession to ready the people for a return home, and he pleads with God to act mercifully for his glory in rescuing his people from their sin and exile (9:1-19). God answers Daniel by sending Gabriel to give a prophetic revelation. Gabriel tells Daniel that exile will actually last seventy times seven years, or four hundred ninety years, and exile will not end until the Messiah comes and is crucified—that is when sin will finally be dealt with and righteousness will be brought in. After that, in the final "week" of human history, the antichrist will come, bringing in the great tribulation and desecrating the holy city. But he will be defeated as Daniel 7 and 9 prophesy. There is an already/not-yet reality in this prophecy. There is significant mystery, but there are also divine certainties we can all agree on.

H. C. Leupold calls Daniel 9 "the divine program for the ages" (*Exposition of Daniel*, 406). On that he is correct because it points to and revolves all around the anointed ruler, Messiah Jesus. The text predicts the coming of the Messiah, Jesus of Nazareth, who will abolish sin and establish everlasting righteousness by being "cut off," executed on a Roman cross. And he will come exactly when God promised he would in one of the most amazing prophecies in the whole Bible. Following his death, the city of Jerusalem and the temple will be destroyed, which it was in AD 70 under the Roman general Titus. As Jesus taught in the Olivet Discourse of Matthew 24, this tragic event anticipates and typifies the end of this present evil age and the arrival of a coming ruler, the antichrist. He will persecute God's people and devastate God's land, but his end will come like a flood when the anointed ruler returns and destroys him. All who long for and love the anointed ruler, King Jesus, will experience in all its fullness the salvation blessings of 9:24. Until then, we work and we wait. We serve and we hope. The plan is in place. The clock is ticking. The anointed ruler is on the way!

Reflect and Discuss

1. Daniel again shows himself to be a man of prayer. What kind of prayers does God hear? From whom does God delight to hear?
2. This is a notoriously difficult passage. How should we approach texts like this that can cause so much confusion?
3. Why does God give this prophecy to Daniel at this time?
4. Summarize each of the four major understandings of the seventy sevens. What are the strengths and weaknesses of each?
5. This passage has some things that are clearer and some that are less clear. What are some of the things we can clearly identify in this text?
6. What is it about the seventy sevens that seems to point to the work of the Messiah?
7. What does it mean for the Messiah to be "cut off" (9:26), and why is this detail important for understanding the New Testament?
8. How does this passage reveal both the mercy and the judgment of God?
9. This prophecy covers the vast scope of world history. What does that tell us about God and his power?
10. Knowing that history and the future are in God's hands, and that his plan is sure, how should Christians live until his plan is brought to completion?

The Life and Death Realities of Spiritual Warfare

DANIEL 10:1-21

Main Idea: God's people can be assured of the reality of spiritual warfare around them and God's guaranteed victory over all his enemies.

I. **Spiritual Warfare Involves Divine Action (10:1).**
   A. God reveals his word (divine sovereignty).
   B. Man seeks to understand (human responsibility).

II. **Spiritual Warfare Requires Reinforcements Given through Prayer and Fasting (10:2-3,12).**
   A. God sees our mourning over our sin (10:2-3).
   B. God hears our prayers when they come from a humble heart (10:12).

III. **Spiritual Warfare Can Be Overwhelming in Its Realities (10:4-17).**
   A. The glory of God can drain us of strength (10:4-9).
   B. Spiritual conflict can take our breath away (10:10-17).

IV. **Spiritual Warfare Should Result in Spiritual Refreshment (10:18-21).**
   A. We should receive peace, strength, and courage (10:18-19).
   B. We should receive insight of both earthly and heavenly truth (10:20-21).

Abraham Kuyper (1837–1920), the brilliant journalist, theologian, and prime minister of the Netherlands, once wrote,

> If once the curtain were pulled back, and the spiritual world behind it came to view, it would expose to our spiritual vision a struggle so intense, so convulsive, sweeping everything within its range, that the fiercest battle ever fought on earth would seem, by comparison, a mere game. Not here, but up there— that is where the real conflict is waged. Our earthly struggle drones in its backlash. (Ferguson, *Daniel*, 199)

Such a bold and striking claim finds biblical warrant when we come to Daniel 10 and the beginning of the end of this marvelous book. Daniel 10–12 constitutes the finale of this prophetic gem. Chapter 10 is the prelude to the detailed vision of chapter 11. Chapter 12 provides the fitting conclusion to both the vision and the book. Chapter 10 pulls back the spiritual curtain and gives us a brief glimpse into a world of spiritual warfare that is very real, though it rages unseen to the physical eye.

I confess to being convicted, even haunted, by this chapter. If the words of this chapter are true, and I believe they are, why do I not pray more? Why do I not pray with more passion and earnestness? Our prayers provide spiritual reinforcement for the battles that take place "against evil, spiritual forces in the heavens" (Eph 6:12). Our prayers are weapons of warfare that provide ammunition for angels as they engage the demonic forces of evil in spiritual combat. Our prayers matter. They make a difference in this unseen but certain world of the spiritual.

I will walk us through this text, making four major observations about certain truths concerning the realities of spiritual warfare. God does not reveal to us everything our curious minds would like to know. However, he does reveal to us everything we need to know.

Spiritual Warfare Involves Divine Action
DANIEL 10:1

The year is approximately 536 BC, "the third year of King Cyrus of Persia" and the third year following his conquest and victory over Babylon and Belshazzar as recorded in Daniel 5. This places the events of chapter 10 two years after the vision of chapter 9.

Darius the Mede (9:1) and King Cyrus of Persia (10:1) are likely the same person. The one man is simply acknowledged and recognized in different but complementary ways. Darius is probably a dynastic title while Cyrus was his proper name. Interestingly, Darius means "he possesses" or "rich and kingly." This fits with the idea that it was a title (Miller, *Daniel*, 174–75). Daniel once more provides a clear and specific historical marker for what takes place.

God Reveals His Word (Divine Sovereignty)

The initiative for the vision of this chapter, as with all true visions, is divine; it is with the Lord. "A message was revealed to Daniel, who was named Belteshazzar." And because the word came from God, it "was true." Verse 1 then adds the interesting comment that it "was about a great conflict." This refers to the content of the vision and the spiritual warfare that was involved in Daniel's receiving an answer to his prayer. The New International Version actually translates it this way: "It concerned a great war." It involves the stress and suffering Daniel will experience in receiving the vision. It also "includes the severe suffering for the people of God (e.g., 11:29-35; see also 12:1)" (Davis, *Message of Daniel*, 140). God takes the initiative to reveal himself and his Word to his "treasured" servant (10:11,19). It is a painful but necessary word.

Man Seeks to Understand (Human Responsibility)

God took the initiative to give Daniel the vision. Still, Daniel had to respond to what he was given, and he did exactly that. The text tells us, "He understood the message and had understanding of the vision." Verse 12 informs us that his understanding came in response to his steadfast, passionate, and humble prayers to God. He set his heart to understand, and God honored him with understanding. Jeremiah 29:13 wonderfully reminds us, "You will seek me and find me when you search for me with all your heart." Daniel sought the Lord, and the Lord answered. Our God is present, and he is not silent. We should be exceedingly thankful that we serve and worship a talking God!

Spiritual Warfare Requires Reinforcements Given through Prayer and Fasting
DANIEL 10:2-3,12

If we were asked to describe the prophet and statesman named Daniel, I think that would be easy. Daniel was a man of prayer. He prayed in chapter 2 that he might be able to interpret Nebuchadnezzar's dream. We know he prayed three times a day in chapter 6 and was thrown into the lions' den for it. He prayed for understanding of a vision. We have his awesome prayer of confession and intercession in chapter 9. Now we see him in fervent prayer once again in chapter 10. Daniel knew we serve a God who listens to the prayers of his beloved children. Once more we find the man of God on his knees, pleading with the heavenly Father.

God Sees Our Mourning over Our Sin (10:2-3)

"In those days" is clarified by verse 4. It was around the time of Passover and the Feast of Unleavened Bread. However, Ezra 1:1-4 provides additional insight. Cyrus has issued a decree allowing the Jews to return home to Israel and Jerusalem. Unfortunately, the number who returned was small, and opposition arose almost immediately to the rebuilding programs. Daniel was not there, having remained in Babylon (perhaps because of old age or to assist through support, encouragement, and prayer); nevertheless, he had received reports from the homeland. His heart was heavy, so he went into mourning for three weeks (v. 2). He also chose not to anoint himself with body oils that would soothe and refresh his skin in that dry climate. Whether he did this publicly or privately we do not know. What we do know is that God heard his prayers and saw his humiliation.

God Hears Our Prayers When They Come from a Humble Heart (10:12)

Verse 12 is fascinating on a number of levels. First, God heard Daniel's prayer the moment he prayed. He sent an answer immediately. Why? Because Daniel had humbled himself before his God. He knew God was in control. He also knew he had nowhere else to turn. He knew that God was sovereign, but he also knew prayer makes a difference. He might not be able to explain the mysterious dance of divine sovereignty and human responsibility, but he knew it was real.

Corrie ten Boom said,

> We never know how God will answer our prayers, but we can expect that He will get us involved in His plan for the answer. If we are true intercessors, we must be ready to take part in God's work on behalf of the people for whom we pray. (Newell, *Expect Great Things*, 224)

And Dee Duke adds,

> Almost everyone believes that prayer is important. But there is a difference between believing that prayer is important and believing it is essential. "Essential" means there are things that will not happen without prayer. (Newell, *Expect Great Things*, 225)

Daniel believed prayer was essential. He was convinced certain things would not happen if he was not on his knees in humble intercession before his God.

Spiritual Warfare Can Be Overwhelming in Its Realities
DANIEL 10:4-17

Several years ago it was popular to talk about "territorial spirits," demons assigned to particular regions, governments, and institutions. Peter Wagner of Fuller Seminary wrote a book titled *Engaging the Enemy: How to Fight and Defeat Territorial Spirits* (Regal, 1991). While some have run the risk of preoccupation and speculation about angels and demons, we play the fool if we make light of or ignore this spiritual reality. Daniel 10 makes clear that (1) angels and demons exist, (2) angels and demons engage one another in spiritual combat, (3) certain demons, and probably certain angels, are given particular geographical and governmental assignments, and (4) our prayers in some genuine measure enter into and affect the battles being fought. John Piper would agree with my theological assessment and summarizes it well:

> I would conclude that there are high-ranking demonic powers
> over various regimes and dominions and governments and
> realms of the world; and that they work to create as much evil
> and corruption and spiritual darkness as they can. They strive
> to interrupt Christian missions and ministry as much as they
> can. ("Angels and Prayer")

The Glory of God Can Drain Us of Strength (10:4-9)

It is ten days after Passover, the twenty-fourth day of the first month of the new year (Boice, *Daniel*, 104). Daniel is standing along the riverbank of the Tigris, approximately twenty miles from the capital city of Babylon (10:4). Suddenly, he looks up and sees a majestic figure who is described in detail in verses 5-6. He looks like a man, but he is clearly more than a man. Many students of Scripture believe he is an angel. This is understandable and the more popular opinion. However, the description of this person is similar to that of the exalted and glorified Lord Jesus in Revelation 1:12-16. I am convinced that this is a Christophany, a preincarnate appearance of the Son of God (cf. Dan 3:25). I also believe the person we see here is to be distinguished from the angel of verse 10. Bryan Chappell makes a similar assessment:

> Who is being described? Clearly this is the Christ, the anointed
> Son of Man, who represents the glory and purposes of God.
> There are many intentional reflections between the chief

figures in these chapters of Daniel and Revelation. The men described in both are clothed in white robes—priestly garb; both have a gold belt—kingly apparel. Both have blazing eyes, both have bronze skin, both have roaring voices—all supernatural traits. In Revelation, the one described holds seven stars in his hand and his face blazes like the sun. Perhaps that explains why the appearance of the man in linen to Daniel makes the prophet faint dead away and causes his friends to run away. The one who comes as a spokesman for God is most readily understood as the Son of God, the Second Person of the Godhead who made the heavens and earth. (*Gospel According to Daniel*, 171–72)

The vision of the glorified Christ in verses 5-6 is overwhelming to Daniel and those who were with him. It appears Daniel saw the vision, but his companions only heard it. Still, just hearing it was enough to scare them to death and cause them to run and hide (v. 7). Daniel was left alone, and he was undone by the vision (v. 8). He was wiped out and drained physically of all his strength. Hearing the words of the vision finished him off. It basically knocked him out cold as he "fell into a deep sleep, with [his] face to the ground" (v. 9; cf. 8:18). Like Isaiah (Isa 6), he could not handle the vision. He was overwhelmed. Undone. Wiped out. Comatose! Ligon Duncan is right: "In the Bible, intimacy with God always leaves its mark" ("The Vision of the Man").

Spiritual Conflict Can Take Our Breath Away (10:10-17)

Daniel is awakened by the touch of a hand (v. 10). I believe this is an angel and a different person from the one described in verses 5-6, who is the Son of God. The angel raised him "trembling" (ESV) to his hands and knees, and Daniel next receives words of encouragement and insight. He is encouraged as he is told he is "a man treasured by God" (v. 11; also 19) and that he should stand up because the angel was sent to him. Of course, this causes him to start trembling again (v. 11). Poor guy! The angel encourages him not to be afraid because from the first day Daniel began to pray the angel was commissioned to come with an answer to Daniel's prayer. God saw his humble heart, heard his words of mourning and intercession, and dispatched his servant angel with an answer (v. 12).

However, a problem arose that delayed the angel's arrival with an answer. A demon, called "the prince of the kingdom of Persia" (v. 13), got in the way and delayed the answer's arrival for twenty-one days.

Only when "Michael, one of the chief princes, came to help" could the angel break free from "the kings of Persia" (note the plural). This angel, possibly Gabriel (cf. 8:15-16; 9:21; Luke 1:19,26-27), had been ganged up on by a number of demons. He therefore needed the aid of the archangel Michael (Jude 9), Israel's protector and prince (Dan 10:21), to continue on his way with an answer to Daniel's prayer. Stephen Miller notes,

> Michael is introduced in this verse and is also mentioned in Dan. 10:21; 12:1; Jude 9; and Rev. 12:7 in Scripture. In Jude 9 he is called the "archangel," which means "first (chief) angel." Michael has been assigned by God as Israel's prince (cf. 10:21); he is "great" in power and protects the Jewish people (cf. 12:1). The implications of these statements are clear. Israel has a mighty angelic supporter in the heavenly realm. Therefore, regardless of Israel's political, military, and economic weaknesses, its existence is assured because no earthly power can resist their great prince." (*Daniel*, 285)

With the aid of Michael, and also the continued prayers of Daniel, the angel has arrived "to help [Daniel] understand what will happen to [his] people [Israel] in the last days"—events that precede and include the coming of God's kingdom (v. 14). The angel's message is clearly going to be eschatological; it is "for days yet to come" (ESV).

Once more Daniel gets more than he can handle, as verse 15 makes clear. The angel speaks, Daniel goes down, and *now* he is "speechless." He can't even respond to what he has heard. Then in verse 16, he is assisted by the angel who touches his lips to open his mouth and enables him to speak. Daniel can talk but nothing more. Pain has come over him, strength has left him, and he can barely breathe (vv. 16-17). He has said all he can. He has nothing left. Dale Davis says it well: "One might wonder if this helpless, sleeping, shaking, speechless, breathless man will ever be in shape to receive the angel's vision" (*Message of Daniel*, 144).

Spiritual Warfare Should Result in Spiritual Refreshment
DANIEL 10:18-21

When it comes to spiritual warfare and the discipline of prayer, Chuck Swindoll makes five insightful observations:

- Believers' prayers are immediately heard by God.
- Demonic forces can delay answers to prayer.

- Wrestling in prayer is exhausting work.
- Following wearisome times in prayer, strength returns in extra measure.
- Overcoming demonic forces is not a once-and-for-all matter. (*Daniel*, 98–101)

Spiritual warfare is not for the weak of heart and the weak in faith. You will be out of your league and well below the cutoff line. Even spiritual giants like Daniel can be overcome and overwhelmed. They can be literally be knocked off their feet and knocked unconscious. They can be drained of all strength and left without a breath. Their lives can feel like they are ebbing away because in their own strength, they are no match for this spiritual arena. Yet, because they are greatly loved of God, help is sent and their energy is renewed. God may knock them down for his sanctifying work, but he promises he will lift them back up (Jas 4:6,10).

We Should Receive Peace, Strength, and Encouragement (10:18-19)

For the third time Daniel is touched by this heavenly visitor (10:10,16,18). The angel's touch strengthens him, restoring his vitality (v. 18). He is told a second time that he is the object of God's great love (vv. 11,19; cf. 9:23). Then the angel delivers to Daniel a threefold message: (1) fear not, (2) peace be with you, and (3) be strong.

Daniel was strengthened (three times in 10:18-19), and he invites the angelic messenger to speak because he has received the spiritual energy necessary to receive and understand his message. Strong words of divine revelation (like ch. 11) require spiritual vitality to receive and embrace them. Daniel got what he needed. He is now ready to hear them. The question for you and me is, Are we ready to hear what God has to say to us no matter what the message might be?

We Should Receive Insight of Both Earthly and Heavenly Truth (10:20-21)

The angel asks Daniel a rhetorical question: "Do you know why I've come to you?" The answer had already been given, at least in part, in verses 12 and 14. Parenthetically, the angel informs Daniel that he has to return to fight against the prince of Persia. The Persian Empire lasted from 539 to 331 BC. After he battles the Persian demons, he will then engage the evil, spiritual forces of Greece. That empire would exist, in some form, from 331 to 63 BC. As with Persia, evil powers would be working for

Greece in the unseen world, engaging the good forces (angels) of God in a battle for the kingdoms of this world and for the souls of men.

Before he leaves for a second deployment, the angel informs Daniel that he will tell him "what is recorded in the book of truth" (v. 21). What an apt description for God's written revelation. Specifically, as chapter 11 makes clear, the revelation details God's plan for Israel and the kingdoms of this world. Before he leaves, he provides one final word: as I go to fight on Israel's behalf, only "Michael, your prince," is with me. Why? Was it because no one else was courageous enough? The CSB would support this view. I prefer a different understanding. God has an untold number of angels to do his bidding. A lack of courage never appears to be a problem for them. No, the reason is because no one else was needed. Gabriel and Michael would be more than sufficient to carry out God's plans and purposes.

Conclusion: How Does This Text Point to Christ?

John Piper, in commenting on Daniel 10, says,

> Take the supernatural seriously and realize that we are in a warfare that cannot and should not be domesticated by reinterpreting everything in the biblical worldview so that it fits nicely with secular, naturalistic ways of thinking about the world. Be ready for the extraordinary as well as the ordinary ways that evil spirits work. Don't be presumptuous, as though demons were weak; and don't be anxious, as though they were stronger than Jesus. ("Angels and Prayer")

John Piper is right. No follower of Jesus should be anxious about demons. A vision of the glorified Son of God is more than sufficient to sustain us no matter what we may encounter. A vision of the exalted Messiah will give us strength to endure the darkest night or trial.

The vision of Daniel 10:5-6 finds its New Testament counterpart in Revelation 1:12-16. Both are wonderful and faithful portraits of King Jesus. He is our faithful priest clothed in linen with a belt of gold around his waist (10:5). He is our glorious sovereign Lord shining brightly with omniscient eyes burning like flaming torches (v. 6). He is an omnipotent Savior with arms and legs like polished bronze. And because of his awesome power and might, his words, when spoken, are like the roar of thousands and thousands (v. 6).

This is the God who strips us of our strength that he may become our strength. This is the God who knocks us down that he may raise us up with renewed strength, peace, and courage (v. 19). Our God often knocks us down to show us who we are without him. And our God raises us up to show us what we can be in him. There is pain in the process. But joy comes in the morning.

Reflect and Discuss

1. How often do you think about the realities of spiritual warfare? What causes you to recognize these realities?
2. Is revelation always a result of divine initiative? Why or why not?
3. What does Daniel show us about the proper response to divine revelation? How do you respond when you read a difficult message in Scripture?
4. What is the relationship between prayer and spiritual warfare? How can you use your prayers to engage in spiritual battle?
5. Read Ephesians 6:10-20. What does that passage say about spiritual warfare? What does it say about prayer?
6. How can we make sure our prayers are humble? Why is this so important?
7. This passage teaches that angels and demons are engaged in combat with one another. Why do you think this is so difficult for many people to believe or understand in our day?
8. Have you ever been overcome by the weightiness of a message from God? If so, how has God also encouraged you in those times?
9. Daniel is encouraged because he is treasured by God. Reflect on God's love for you as shown in Christ (Rom 5:8). How can this encourage you as you encounter spiritual opposition?
10. Read Daniel 10:5-6 and Revelation 1:12-16. What similarities do you see?

Civil War: Just as God Said It Would Happen

DANIEL 11:1-20

Main Idea: God knows about the future in advance and reigns sovereign over the rise and fall of all kingdoms great and small, directing history according to his providential plan.

I. **God Raised Up Medo-Persia and Greece According to His Plan and Purposes (11:1-4).**
   A. God supports and protects as he chooses (11:1-2).
   B. God breaks and divides as he chooses (11:3-4).
II. **God Raised Up Egypt and Syria According to His Plan and Purposes (11:5-20).**
   A. God gave Egypt victory, but its king exalted himself (11:5-12).
   B. God gave Syria victory, but its king was willful and insolent (11:13-20).

In James 4:1-2, the Bible says,

> What is the source of wars and fights among you? Don't they come from your passions that wage war within you? You desire and do not have. You murder and covet and cannot obtain. You fight and wage war. You ask and don't receive because you ask with wrong motives.

Lust for power, lust for prestige, lust for possessions—a bloodlust for more is a dark cloud that has cast its ominous shadow over the totality of human history going all the way back to Genesis 4 and the story of Cain and Abel. Daniel 11 gives us more of the same.

Daniel 10–12 is a unit, and it gives us the final vision of this remarkable book of prophecy. It gives us a glimpse of the history that takes place between the Old and New Testaments, what is sometimes called the four hundred silent years. Chapter 10 provides the context. Chapter 11 contains the content. Chapter 12 is the conclusion.

Chapter 11 is a remarkable passage for a number of different reasons. Because of its unique content some, like H. C. Leupold, do not think it can be preached in a sermon (*Exposition of Daniel*, 525). It might be OK for a Bible study but not proclamation. On the other hand, because of its detailed and accurate description of history, more liberal scholars have denied its prophetic nature, arguing that a second-century author simply recorded past history and passed it off as prophecy. There is a technical, theological term for this: *vaticinium ex eventu,* which means "prophecy from or after the event."

My response to these two claims is simple and straightforward. First, since all Scripture is divinely inspired, then all Scripture, including Daniel 11, should be preached. It may be more challenging than a Pauline letter, but it still should be proclaimed. I basically agree with James Boice:

> Even though the eleventh chapter is difficult, it calls for
> a detailed explanation. . . . This is the last, longest, most
> detailed, and therefore most important, prophecy in the book.
> (*Daniel,* 111)

Second, the issue of prophecy comes down to the supernatural and the nature of God. If the God of the Bible is omniscient—knowing all things past, present, and future—then even highly detailed predictive prophecy like Daniel 11 is not a problem. Sinclair Ferguson is right:

> What is at stake then is a vital issue: Does God so rule history
> and can He so communicate with us that His future purposes
> may be disclosed to us before the events? (*Daniel,* 204)

It is my conviction, rooted in a supernatural worldview, that this chapter is a bona fide prophecy of future events. God inspired it, the angel revealed it, Daniel wrote it, and we get to read and interpret it!

The first twenty verses of Daniel 11, the object of our study, break down into two uneven divisions examining four kingdoms: (1) Medo-Persia and Greece in 11:1-4, and (2) Egypt and Syria in 11:5-20. How these kingdoms relate to God's people, the nation of Israel, is always the backdrop and interest of Daniel.

God Raised Up Medo-Persia and Greece According to His Plan and Purposes
DANIEL 11:1-4

Four great empires, in relation to Israel, were described in Daniel 2 and 7: Babylon, Medo-Persia, Greece, and Rome. In Daniel 8 the vision narrows the focus to two: Medo-Persia and Greece. Those same two empires are the interest of the angel at the beginning of Daniel 11. However, this time they do not get a chapter. They only get four verses.

God Supports and Protects as He Chooses (11:1-2)

Daniel 11:1 is a hinge verse that connects chapter 10 with chapter 11. The angel of chapter 10 (possibly Gabriel) informs Daniel that he came on the scene "to strengthen and protect" Darius the Mede (Cyrus) in the first year of his reign (539 BC). This is two years before the vision of chapters 10–12 (cf. 10:1). This is important because that same year Cyrus issued a decree allowing the Jews to return to Israel. Perhaps God used Gabriel to strengthen Darius to issue the decree.

Verse 2 begins our lengthy history lesson. It also contains a divine affirmation: "Now I will tell you the truth." Following Darius, "three more kings will arise in Persia." History records that these three kings were Cambyses (530–522 BC), Smerdis (522 BC), and Darius I Hystapes (522–486 BC). Then a fourth will arise who is "far richer than the others." This king will also provoke Greece and set the stage for the rise of the Greek Empire. His name was Xerxes I (486–465 BC). He would invade Greece with a mighty army but be defeated in the Battle of Salamis in 480 BC. And with that we are finished with Persia. God used it to send Israel back home. It did its job. To the dustbin of history it goes. God supported and protected it to accomplish his chosen purpose.

God Breaks and Divides as He Chooses (11:3-4)

There is a 150-year gap between verses 2 and 3. What happened in that period is not important for the story God wishes to reveal in this vision. Scholars agree that the "warrior king" (ESV, "mighty king") of verse 3 is the Greek Alexander the Great (336–323 BC). Historians have written volumes about him. God gives him one verse in this chapter! He was a powerful king who conquered the known world of his day and ruled with absolute power. He indeed did whatever he wanted. But he died at age thirty-three. So,

> *as soon as he is established, his kingdom will be broken up and divided to the four winds of heaven, but not to his descendants; it will not be the same kingdom that he ruled, because his kingdom will be uprooted and will go to others besides them.* (v. 4)

This is precisely what happened. Alexander's sons were murdered, and no part of his vast empire went to his descendants. As we mentioned earlier, following his death, four of his generals divided up his kingdom into four parts:

- Cassander took Macedonia and Greece.
- Lysimachus took Thrace and portions of Asia Minor.
- Ptolemy took Egypt and Israel.
- Seleucus took Syria and Mesopotamia.

However, none of these kingdoms ever came close to matching the power and strength of Alexander's brief empire. God plucked Alexander's kingdom up, divided it into four pieces, and gave to others as he saw fit. And with that the great Alexander is finished. He served God's plan and purposes. Off he goes!

God Raised Up Egypt and Syria According to His Plan and Purposes
DANIEL 11:5-20[6]

Bob Fyall (*Daniel*, 167) provides a nice list of the cast of characters for Daniel 11:5-35:

The South (Ptolemies in Egypt)	The North (Seleucids in Syria)
Ptolemy I (Soter) 323–285	Seleucus I (Nicator) 312–280
Ptolemy II (Philadelphus) 285–246	Antiochus I (Soter) 280–261
Ptolemy III (Euergetes) 246–221	Antiochus II (Theos) 261–246
Ptolemy IV (Philopator) 221–203	Seleucus II (Callinicus) 246–226
Ptolemy V (Epiphanes) 203–181	Seleucus III (Ceraunus) 226–223
Ptolemy VI (Philometor) 181–145	Antiochus III (Magnus) 223–187
	Seleucus IV (Philopator) 187–175
	Antiochus IV (Epiphanes) 175–163

In the grand scheme of world history, Egypt and Syria don't amount to much during this period of time (ca. 323–163 BC). The more significant global power is Rome, the new "bad boy" arising in the background. However, the reason Egypt and Syria receive all the press here is because

---

[6] The exposition of verses 5-20 is heavily dependent on Miller, *Daniel*, 293–97.

they are important in their relationship to Israel and the people of God. They will play political ping-pong with the nation of Israel for almost 175 years until the evil, antichrist-type figure Antiochus IV Epiphanes (175–163 BC) comes on the scene. That is the subject of verses 20-45. Until then, ongoing civil war takes place between Egypt and Syria with Israel tragically caught in the middle.

God Gave Egypt Victory, but Its King Exalted Himself (11:5-12)

Verses 5-12 record the period of Ptolemaic or Egyptian dominance. "The king of the South" (v. 5) is a reference to Ptolemy I Soter (323–285 BC), the ruler of Egypt and a general under Alexander. "One of his commanders" alludes to Seleucus I Nicator (312/311–280 BC), who fled (in 316 BC) to Ptolemy Soter to serve under him, but later abandoned him and returned to the northern kingdom. There he greatly increased his power, eventually controlling more territory than Ptolemy. His kingdom included Babylonia, Syria, and Media, the largest of all the divisions of the Greek Empire.

Conflicts would continue between the kingdoms of the Ptolemies (Egypt) and the Seleucids (Syria). Ptolemy I died in 285 BC, and war continued under his son Ptolemy II Philadelphus (285–246 BC), who according to tradition commissioned the translation of the Hebrew Bible into Greek—called the Septuagint (abbreviated LXX). Finally, Ptolemy II made a treaty of peace with the Seleucid ruler, Antiochus II Theos (261–246 BC, grandson of Seleucus) around 250 BC. Verse 6 refers to this alliance.

Berenice, Ptolemy's daughter ("the daughter of the king of the South"), was arranged to marry Antiochus ("the king of the North") "to seal the agreement" between the two kingdoms (v. 6). Marriages for political expediency have been going on for a long time. However, Antiochus was already married to a woman named Laodice. The former wife and woman scorned took revenge and succeeded in murdering Antiochus, Berenice, and their child. Berenice, therefore, "will not retain power."

Verse 7 refers to Berenice's brother, Ptolemy III Euergetes (246–221 BC), who succeeded his father, Philadelphus, to the throne of Egypt. In retaliation for his sister's murder, Ptolemy III attacked Syria ("the king of the North") with a great army. This war lasted from 246 to 241 BC. Ptolemy captured and looted the Seleucid capital of Antioch, "the fortress of the king of the North." Ptolemy seized Syria's "gods" and other valuables (v. 8). He also returned to Egypt with treasures, including sacred idols that had been taken by the Persian monarch Cambyses in 524 BC.

"The king of the North" is the subject of verse 9. Apparently (we have no further information) he attempted an invasion of Egypt, but the campaign was brief. He would "return to his own land."

The Syrian king Seleucus II died in 226 BC, but his sons, Seleucus III Ceraunus (226–223 BC) and Antiochus III (the Great; 223–187 BC), continued the conflicts with the Ptolemies (v. 10). Seleucus III was murdered after a brief three-year reign, and his brother Antiochus III came to power. He was called "the Great" because of his military successes, and in 219–218 BC he campaigned in Phoenicia and Palestine, part of the Ptolemaic Empire ("as far as [the king of the South's] fortress").

In response, the "infuriated" (v. 11) Ptolemy IV Philopater (221–203 BC) launched a counterattack. Ptolemy would win a great victory over Antiochus and the Syrians at Raphia (in Palestine) in 217 BC. Because of this victory, Ptolemy "will become arrogant" (v. 12). The Egyptian army slaughtered "tens of thousands" of the Syrian troops in the battle, though the Ptolemaic triumph would not continue.

The text implies in verse 11 that God gave the king of the South, Egypt, its victory. However, as the human heart is so easily inclined to do, the Egyptian king became "arrogant," and his heart was "exalted" (v. 12 ESV). He became proud, and we all know how God deals with proud men and women!

God Gave Syria Victory, but Its King Was Willful and Insolent (11:13-20)

Verse 13 and following change direction and describe the period of Seleucid supremacy. Approximately fifteen years after the Egyptians slaughtered the Syrians (202 BC), Antiochus III again invaded Ptolemaic territories with a huge army (v. 13). The occasion for this invasion was the death of Ptolemy IV in 203 BC and the crowning of his four- to six-year-old son, Ptolemy V Epiphanes (203–181 BC), as the new Egyptian ruler.

Among those who "will rise up against the king of the South" (v. 14) were Philip V of Macedon and revolutionaries within Egypt. There were also "violent ones among [Daniel's] own people," which here refers to those Jews who aided Antiochus. These Israelites "will assert themselves" against Egypt "to fulfill a vision," possibly the prophecy recorded here. The fulfillment of the prediction was not the intention of these persons, but it was nevertheless the result. "But [those who sided with Antiochus] will fail." Their defeat came at the hands of the Egyptian General Scopas, who was himself eventually defeated. Antiochus III's Syrian forces advanced against Egypt at the Battle of Panium (now called Banian, near the area of the Caesarea Philippi mentioned in the Gospels) in 199 BC and won a resounding victory (v. 15). They pursued the Egyptians south and captured Sidon, the "well-fortified city," where General Scopas finally surrendered in 198 BC. The South had suffered a decisive defeat at the hands of the North.

With the defeat of the Egyptians at Sidon, Antiochus acquired complete control over Phoenicia and Palestine, and he "will do whatever he wants" (v. 16). Indeed "no one can oppose him." Although Palestine had come under Antiochus's control for a brief time previously (ca. 219–217 BC), it would now become a permanent possession of the Syrian Empire. The phrase "with total destruction in his hand" emphasizes Antiochus III's complete power over the "beautiful land" (cf. 8:9; Ezek 20:6). David Helm reminds us,

> Earlier in Daniel we came across the phrase "the glorious [beautiful] land" (8:9) and we will see it again in this chapter (11:41). In both instances it refers to Israel, to Jerusalem and the city of God. (*Daniel for You,* 192)

This is important because it sets the stage for the reign of terror to follow under the Syrian Greek ruler Antiochus IV Epiphanes (175–164 BC).

The Syrians forced terms of peace on the Egyptian king (v. 17). To seal the deal, Antiochus gave his daughter Cleopatra (not the Cleopatra who married Mark Antony over a hundred years later) to Ptolemy V as a wife. Antiochus hoped that through Cleopatra he could gain further control of Egypt. However, his plan did not succeed. Cleopatra loved her husband more than her father and supported the Egyptian cause completely.

Verses 18-19 prophesy Antiochus's defeat and ignominious end. Having defeated the Egyptians in 197 BC or shortly thereafter, Antiochus turned "his attention to the coasts and islands," or countries around the Mediterranean. After Antiochus had some initial success, Lucius Cornelius Scipio was sent against him by the Roman government. This is the commander who "will put an end to his taunting; instead, he will turn his taunts against him." In 191 BC the Romans, fighting with their Greek allies, routed the Syrians at Thermopylae and forced them to withdraw from Greece and flee to Asia Minor. Thirty thousand Roman troops pursued Antiochus into Asia and defeated his much larger army of seventy thousand at the Battle of Magnesia near Smyrna (Turkey) in 190 BC. After this humiliating defeat, Antiochus returned to his country, where he was killed by an angry mob in 187 BC as he sought to pillage the temple of Zeus (Bel) at Elymais (11:19). He indeed stumbled, fell, and was no more.

The son and successor of Antiochus III was Seleucus IV Philopator (187–175 BC), who sent a "tax collector" (Heliodorus) to collect money to pay the thousand-talent indemnity demanded annually by the Romans as part of the settlement for Syria's surrender to Rome (v. 20). Seleucus IV reigned only a few years and was not killed by an angry mob ("in anger") like his father or "in battle." Heliodorus, his tax collector and prime minister, evidently seeking to gain the throne for himself, poisoned the king (possibly aided by Antiochus IV).

The stage is set for the antichrist figure Antiochus IV Epiphanes in verses 21-35. History has unfolded just as God said it would. Kingdoms and their despots come and go. They live and die. They win and lose. And our great God in heaven watches it all and laughs (Ps 2:4)!

Conclusion

This is an unusual and unique passage to be sure. God is never mentioned by name, and there is a lot of unfamiliar imagery for our Western twenty-first-century minds to grasp. Asking five basic theological and practical questions (which we should ask in some manner of every text) can help us get at what God wants us to understand from this portion of the Bible that he inspired.

What Does This Text Teach Us about God?

Our God is sovereign and omniscient, knowing the future to the smallest detail. He can predict the future with pinpoint accuracy. Back in Daniel 4:17 we were taught, "The Most High is ruler over human kingdoms. He gives [them] to anyone he wants and sets the lowliest of people over [them]." He is the one breaking and dividing and uprooting in chapter 11, verse 4. These earthly rulers are mere pawns in the sovereign hands of an omnipotent and providential God.

What Does This Text Teach Us about Fallen Humanity?

Man in his depravity, pride, and sin has a bloodlust for power and possessions. He fights and wars, doing "whatever he wants" if he can. Might makes right. Man exalts his heart and inflates his sense of self-worth. Given the opportunity, he will trample over others with little or no regard for those who get hurt in the process. This is the story of human history since the fall, and it will continue to be our legacy until the return of God's King and the inauguration of his kingdom.

What Does This Text Teach Us about Christ?

This passage and the one that follows (11:21-45) must be read in the context of Daniel 7:13-14 and 9:24-27. There we see the Son of Man coming in glory to receive from the Ancient of Days a kingdom that will not pass away or ever be destroyed. His kingdom is not a fly-by-night empire that is here today and gone tomorrow, an empire and kingdom that is little more than dust in the wind! Further, the anointed ruler of Daniel 9 does what no piddly, earthly potentate can do. He brings rebellion to an end, puts a stop to sin, wipes away iniquity, and brings in everlasting righteousness. What a contrast are these power hungry dictators with the humble King from Galilee who put the needs of others far ahead of his own.

What Does God Want Me to Know?

In Christ pride gives way to humility, and wanting more and more gives way to giving and serving others. A passion to build my kingdom gives way to a passion to build God's kingdom!

What Does God Want Me to Do?

Learn from the mistakes and sins of men and women from the past who pursued earthly gain and not heavenly reward. Avoid the pitfalls of pride and greed; instead, pursue Christ and his traits of humility, generosity, and service. You won't act, look, or live like the kings of Daniel 11. You will, however, begin to look and live more and more like the King of kings and Lord of lords.

Reflect and Discuss

1. How does the Bible show God's relationship to history? How does this differ from the naturalistic view of history?
2. Do you think passages like this are suitable for preaching and teaching in the local church? Why or why not?
3. Why do some liberal scholars believe this passage was recorded in the second century BC? What assumptions and presuppositions lead them to that conclusion?
4. Why does God sometimes uphold evil empires?
5. Identify the major nations described in this chapter. What is the fate of each of them?
6. Identify each of the major individuals in this chapter. What is the fate of each of them?
7. Reflect on the five theological application questions we should ask of every text. Write your own answers to each of them.
8. Read Daniel 11 in the context of Daniel 10 and 12. How does it fit into the vision as a whole?
9. Discuss the striking contrast of the kingdom of God in Daniel 7 with the kingdoms of man in Daniel 10.
10. Why does God raise up evil kingdoms? How does this help us get a biblical perspective when it happens in our own day?

Antiochus Epiphanes and the Antichrist: The Archenemies of God's People

DANIEL 11:21-45

Main Idea: God reigns sovereign over the greatest enemies of his people and even uses those enemies for his own purposes.

I. **God Raised Up a Contemptible Person to Refine, Purify, and Sanctify His People (11:21-35).**
   A. Beware of using flattery and deceit (11:21-24).
   B. Guard your heart and tongue (11:25-28).
   C. Embrace God's work in spite of difficulty and suffering (11:29-35).

II. **God Will Raise Up the Antichrist, Who Will Exalt and Magnify Himself as God (11:36-45).**
   A. He will deify himself (11:36-39).
   B. He will be a man of unbridled conquest (11:40-45).

He goes by many names and has had many forerunners throughout history. In the Bible he is called the "little horn" (Dan 7:9), "coming ruler" (Dan 9:26), "man of lawlessness" (2 Thess 2:3), "man doomed to destruction" (2 Thess 2:3), and "beast" (Rev 13:1-10). We know him most popularly as the "antichrist" (1 John 2:18,22; 4:2-3; 2 John 7). He is the spirit of this present evil age, and he is an eschatological, apocalyptic figure who will build a global empire and "exalt and magnify himself above every god, and he will say outrageous things against the God of gods" (Dan 11:36). He is a self-centered, arrogant, prideful, egomaniacal individual who epitomizes the depravity of man and our longing to be like God (Gen 3).

What people think about the antichrist varies. In a LifeWay Research article titled "Pastors: The End of the World Is Complicated," it was reported that

> most Protestant pastors believe Jesus will return in the
> future. But few agree about the details of the apocalypse. A
> third of America's Protestant pastors expect Christians to be
> raptured—or taken up in the sky to meet Jesus—as the end

times begin. About half think a false messiah known as the
Antichrist will appear sometime in the future. A surprising
number think the Antichrist has already been here or isn't on
his way at all. . . . About half (49 percent) say the Antichrist
is a figure who will arise in the future. Others say there is no
individual Antichrist (12 percent); that, he is a personification
of evil (14 percent) or an institution (7 percent). Six percent
say the Antichrist has already been here. Baptists (75 percent)
and Pentecostals (83 percent) are most likely to see a future
Antichrist. Lutherans (29 percent), Methodists (28 percent),
and Presbyterian/Reformed pastors (31 percent) are more
likely to see the Antichrist as a personification of evil.
Education also played a role in how pastors see the Antichrist.
Two-thirds of those with no college degree (68 percent) or a
bachelor's (63 percent) believe in a future Antichrist figure.
Fewer than half of those with a master's (39 percent) or a
doctorate (49 percent) hold that view. (Smietana, "Pastors:
The End of the World Is Complicated")

We see these findings played out, to some degree, in how people
interpret the closing verses of Daniel 11. All scholars without exception,
liberal and conservative, see verses 21-35 as referring to the evil reign of
Antiochus Epiphanes (175–163 BC) and his vicious persecution of the
Hebrews and Israel. But what about verses 36-45? All scholars without
exception, liberal and conservative, agree the events here described
cannot line up with what we know of Antiochus. So most liberal scholars
say the second century pseudo-author of Daniel was so accurate in
11:1-20 because he was writing prophesy after the fact. In 11:36-45,
however, he got sloppy for some unknown reason and made a number
of historical blunders.

Most evangelicals, in contrast, believe this is an example again of
what is called "prophetic foreshortening," where there is a significant
time interval between two verses, between two persons or events (cf. Isa
61:1-2b; Dan 9:24-27 and the gap between verses 26 and 27). The classic
example of this prophetic feature is how the prophets saw the first
and second coming of Christ. The prophets, gazing at two prophetic
mountain peaks in a straight line, did not see the gap (i.e., "the valley")
between the two comings. I am convinced this is what we have between
Antiochus (a type of the antichrist) in verses 21-35 and the antichrist
(the antitype) in verses 36-45. It is important and even decisive to note

the shift in language. Daniel speaks of "the appointed time" in reference to Antiochus in verses 27, 29, and 35. In contrast he uses the phrase "at the time of the end" in verse 40 and throughout chapter 12. This tips us off that we are in a different time period in verses 36-45. Further, Paul uses Daniel 11:36 in 2 Thessalonians 2:3 when talking about the end-time antichrist ("the man of lawlessness"). Sinclair Ferguson notes this perspective

> is also consistent with the way in which Jesus seems to have seen the description of Antiochus' activity as foreshadowing the future. Jesus speaks of an "abomination of desolation" (v. 31) that was yet to come (Mark 13:14). (*Daniel*, 219)

So our text divides into two sections: (1) Antiochus: the type of the coming antichrist (11:20-35), and (2) the antichrist: the final eschatological earthly enemy of God and his people (vv. 36-45).

God Raised Up a Contemptible Person to Refine, Purify, and Sanctify His People
DANIEL 11:21-35

Anti-Semitism and opposition to Israel, which seem to be growing in our day, is not new. It is as old as the Bible and began all the way back in the book of Exodus. However, in the Old Testament, no one epitomizes this evil like the Syrian general and king Antiochus Epiphanes. While there are history lessons here to be sure, significant theological and spiritual truth is embedded throughout for our edification.

Beware of Using Flattery and Deceit (11:21-24)

The "despised person" (ESV, "contemptible person") of verse 21 is Antiochus IV Epiphanes (175–163 BC), who replaced Seleucus IV after the latter died from poisoning (v. 20). This is an apt description of him "because from the Jewish vantage point he was a monster" (Miller, *Daniel*, 298). "Royal honors" rightly belonged to a man named Demetrius I Soter, the son of Seleucus IV. However, Antiochus slithered in "during a time of peace and [seized] the kingdom by intrigue" (ESV, "flatteries"). Political skills wedded to an evil heart are a dangerous combination!

The Egyptian Ptolemy VI Philometor (181–146 BC) attacked Antiochus with "a flood of forces" (v. 22), a large army, but he was soundly defeated ("broken") and taken captive. During this time

Antiochus also deposed Onias III, the rightful high priest in Jerusalem. Here he is called the "covenant prince." Onias was assassinated in 171 BC (Baldwin, *Daniel,* 192).

Verses 23-24 summarize Antiochus's consolidation of power as he continues to use the political and sinful device of deception. He negotiated an alliance with Egypt that he had no intention of honoring (v. 25). With a peace agreement intact, he invaded "the richest parts of the province" (including Egypt and Judea) and did "what his fathers and predecessors never did" (v. 24). He will build his kingdom to greater heights by "[lavishing] plunder, loot, and wealth on his followers." He will buy allegiance. And he would make plans for further conquest ("plans against fortified cities"), but those would only last "for a [short] time." God was raising up mighty Rome, and Antiochus would be no match for this beast that is "frightening and dreadful, and incredibly strong, with large iron teeth" (7:7).

Flattery and deceit only get you so far. They are sinful characteristics God will not bless. They also are no match for the plans of a sovereign God! They are wicked devices his children should avoid at all cost.

Guard Your Heart and Tongue (11:25-28)

These verses appear to refer back to Antiochus's first campaign against Egypt in verse 22 (169 BC). He defeated the king of the South, in part, because "plots [were] made against him" (v. 25). Evil men engaged in evil deeds. Stephen Miller notes these plots against Egypt's king "seem to include Antiochus's plans against him, the activities of disloyal subjects in Egypt, and the poor counsel of his advisers" (*Daniel,* 306). The last observation is confirmed by verse 26 ("Those who eat his provisions will destroy him").

Egypt and Syria sit down at the negotiating table in verse 27, but as is so often the case in political conversations, they do so with "hearts . . . bent on evil," speaking lies to one another "at the same table." Evil hearts speak evil words (Jas 3:5-8). The talks fail; they come "to no avail." Why? Because "the end will come at the appointed time" set by God. Things will move forward on God's timetable, not the timetable of mere humans. Antiochus would return home to Syria "with great wealth" after plundering Egypt in 169 BC.

Upon his return he found a Jewish insurrection in progress, and his heart was "set against the holy covenant" (Israel; 11:28). Stephen Miller writes,

He put down the rebellion, massacring eighty thousand men, women, and children (2 Macc. 5:12-14) and then looted the temple with the help of the evil high priest, Menelaus (cf. 2 Macc. 5:15-21). The persecution of the Jews by this evil tyrant had now escalated to calamitous proportions. (*Daniel*, 300)

Humans out of wicked hearts may lie, intimidate, and negotiate endlessly. They may plot, rebel, murder, and pillage. Still, the final outcome is in God's hands. God controls history. We should watch after our hearts and guard our tongues while trusting that God is at work even in the midst of an evil and out-of-control world.

Embrace God's Work in Spite of Difficulty and Suffering (11:29-35)[7]

We now arrive at the main point and purpose of verses 21-35. It is without question and in many ways "at the appointed time" (v. 29), as the God of history orchestrates his plan for his people (v. 35). Antiochus once again launches a campaign against Egypt (the South), but this time things are different: "This time will not be like the first."

Antiochus encountered opposition from the "Ships of Kittim" (Cyprus), a Roman fleet that had come to Alexandria at the request of the Ptolemies (11:30). The Roman commander Gaius Popilius Laenas met Antiochus and handed him a letter from the Roman Senate ordering him to either leave Egypt or deal with Rome. The Roman commander famously drew a circle in the sand around Antiochus and told him that he must give an answer before stepping out of the circle. Antiochus wisely withdrew from Egypt and headed back to Antioch humiliated (v. 30).

Antiochus's embarrassment turned into anger, which he directed against the Jewish people ("the holy covenant") once more. He sent Apollonius (2 Macc 5:23-26), the head of his mercenaries and the "chief collector of tribute" (1 Macc 1:29), to Jerusalem. Apollonius pretended to come in peace, but on the Sabbath Day he suddenly attacked the Jews, massacring many people and plundering the city (cf. 1 Macc 1:30-32; 2 Macc 5:25-26). But he rewarded those apostate Jews ("those who abandon the holy covenant," Dan 11:30) like the high priest Menelaus, who supported his Hellenizing policies (cf. 1 Macc 1:30-32; 2 Macc 4:7-17) (Miller, *Daniel*, 301).

---

[7] Stephen Miller again is helpful in the historical details, and I acknowledge my heavy dependence on him in this section. Ibid., 301–4.

In 167 BC, the persecution of the Jewish religion reached a climax (1 Macc 1:41-50; 2 Macc 6:1-6). All Jewish religious practices such as circumcision, possessing the Scriptures, offering sacrifices, and observing feast days were forbidden on penalty of death (1 Macc 1:50,63), and the imperial cult was introduced. Desecration of the Jewish religion reached a crescendo on December 15, 167 BC (1 Macc 1:54) when an altar or idol-statue devoted to Zeus was erected in the temple. On December 25, sacrifices including swine (cf. 1 Macc 1:47; 2 Macc 6:4-5) were offered on the altar (cf. 1 Macc 1:54,59). The temple was desecrated, and "the abomination of desolation" became a historical reality (11:31).

Antiochus used "flattery" in order to entice people to support his policies (cf. 1 Macc 2:18; 2 Macc 7:24). This would further "corrupt" the apostate Jews who "act wickedly" (Dan 11:32). Still, even in this dark period there were faithful believers ("the people who know their God"). First Maccabees 1:62-63 (NRSV) speaks of them: "Many in Israel stood firm and were resolved in their hearts not to eat unclean food. They chose to die rather than to be defiled by food or to profane the holy covenant; and they did die."

Stephen Miller further informs us,

> Foremost among those who resisted the oppressive measures
> of Antiochus were the Maccabees. A certain priest named
> Mattathias refused to forsake his God (cf. 1 Macc. 2:1-14).
> He had five sons, three of whom (Judas, Jonathan, and
> Simon) became known as the Maccabees, although the term
> Maccabeus ("hammer") originally was given only to Judas
> (1 Macc. 2:4). The Maccabees successfully overthrew the
> Syrian yoke through a series of brilliant military victories
> (apparently predicted in Zech. 9:13-17) against Antiochus's
> military commanders, Apollonius, Seron, Grogias, Lysias (cf.
> 1 Macc. 3:10–4:35) between 166 [or 165] and 164 B.C.; as a
> result the temple was rededicated (Hanukkah) to Yahweh
> on 25 Chislev (December 14) 164 B.C. (1 Macc. 4:52).
> (*Daniel*, 302)

"Those who have insight" (Dan 11:33) are Israelites who have spiritual discernment, the true believers. They would remain true to Yahweh during Antiochus's persecution and instruct others ("give understanding to many"). Because of their stand, many of the Jewish faithful would be killed. Tens of thousands were slaughtered in these persecutions, and many others died during the fighting. Others were "captured" for slaves or had their property confiscated ("plundered"). Though intense, this persecution would last only for a short while. Some of these faithful heroes seem to be noted in Hebrews 11:34 (Miller, *Daniel*, 303).

During this period of oppression, when they are defeated, those faithful to Yahweh "will be helped by some," presumably a small number of forces who at first fought against Antiochus. The rest of verse 34 appears to refer to the fact that as the strength of the Maccabean revolt grew, nominally committed Jews joined with the rebels out of expediency, particularly when the Maccabean forces (now joined by the Hasidim, a word meaning "pious ones") began to put to death those who had collaborated with the Seleucids (i.e., those loyal to Antiochus; cf. 1 Macc 2:42-48).

"Some of those who have insight will fall" expresses the same idea as verse 33—true believers will suffer persecution and even martyrdom for their faith. The purpose is to refine, purify, and cleanse individuals and the nation as a whole of sinful practices and to strengthen their faith "until the time of the end" (v. 35). In this context this is the time that has been "appointed" by the Lord for the termination of Antiochus's persecutions, not the eschatological end time. Those suffering in the second century BC would have been greatly comforted by the promise of an end to their suffering (Miller, *Daniel*, 303).

Stephen Miller notes,

> Antiochus IV died in 163 BC during an expedition in Persia, bringing to a conclusion both his wicked life and his atrocities against God's people. Antiochus died a horrible death.
> Polybius relates that according to some the king died insane. (Ibid., 304)

The despised king was and is no more.

God Will Raise Up the Antichrist, Who Will Exalt and Magnify Himself as God
DANIEL 11:36-45

There is a gap of undetermined time between verses 35 and 36. We have moved from "appointed times" (vv. 27,29,35) in the past (from our perspective) to the "time of the end" (v. 40; also 12:4,6-7,9,13) and the future. The events described in these verses cannot refer to Antiochus Epiphanes. As arrogant as he was, he never did "exalt and magnify himself above every god" (v. 36). He remained a devoted follower of Zeus until his death. No, the man described here is an end-time personality. He is the antichrist. Daniel highlights two truths for our careful consideration of this archenemy of God.

He Will Deify Himself (11:36-37)

First, the antichrist is a self-willed man. He "will do whatever he wants." He is egomaniacal. Second, "he will exalt and magnify himself above every god." He sees himself as a divine man. Third, "he will say outrageous things against the God of gods." He is a gross blasphemer. Fourth, "he will be successful until the time of wrath [God's judgment] is completed" (ESV, "accomplished"). This is a signed and settled reality "because what has been decreed [by God] will be accomplished." Sinclair Ferguson is spot-on when he says,

> We have already seen this spirit emerge in various figures
> in Daniel (cf. 3:15; 4:30; 8:25; 11:3,12,16). It will emerge
> in full-blown form at the end in the final conflict between
> the kingdoms. It does so inevitably because it is the crux
> of the conflict. Its foundations run back into the origins of
> history and beyond into the mists to eternity. The tempting
> words "you will be like God" echo through the ages from a
> whisper in the Garden of Eden to a clamor at the end of time.
> (*Daniel*, 220)

Verse 37 continues the evil parade of vices that will characterize this anti-God menace. First, "he will not show regard for the gods of his fathers, the god desired by women, or for any other god." This sentence is, if anything, unclear. The first phrase is easier to understand. The antichrist will have no respect for his religious heritage, whatever it might be. But what of "the god desired by women," which is translated in the English Standard Version as "the one beloved by women"? I find the insights of Andrew Steinmann helpful and persuasive. He writes,

> The king will not favor normal marital relations nor any god
> because he will make himself greater than all (11:37). His
> arrogance renders him incapable of the loving devotion that
> is required by both marriage and true piety. He personally is

not married and does not rightly honor the one true God,
and as a king, he imposes this disdain for marriage and this
dishonorable view of God upon his subjects. (*Daniel*, 542)

The antichrist has no desire for God or humanity because he serves
a different god in addition to himself, "a god of fortresses" or the god
of war (v. 38). On this "might makes right" deity, one that even his
evil forefathers did not know or worship, he will shower "gold, silver,
precious stones, and riches." He will honor the might and power that
war can give him. And "with the help of [this] foreign god" (v. 39),
the god even his fathers did not know (v. 38), "he will deal with the
strongest fortresses." With power he will crush power, and in the process
he will reward those who join his expanding coalition. He will "greatly
honor [them], making them rulers over many and distributing land as
a reward" (v. 39). This is a Nietzschean world come to full fruition. The
vision of a Hitler-like leader and his Nietzschean Nazism will arrive in all
of its infamy, and the world will not be able to stop it.

He Will Be a Man of Unbridled Conquest (11:40-45)

Sinclair Ferguson wisely instructs us that "the vision of the future is
presented in terms of the experience, knowledge, and events of the
present" (*Daniel*, 221). This is certainly true for verses 40-44. What is
described here, in the language and perspective of Daniel's day, is the
final struggle or battle "at the time of the end" (11:40). One battle may
be in view or, more likely, a final campaign is being described here.
Giving us precise details is not the vision's goal; the character of the
antichrist and those like him who would rule this temporal and fading
world is. Let's summarize these verses broadly by outline:

- At the end of this age, the antichrist, now identified as "the
  king of the North," will be attacked by "the king of the South,"
  but the antichrist will win a resounding victory (v. 40). This will
  allow him to advance into other countries and "sweep through
  them like a flood."
- He will invade Israel, "the beautiful land," and many will die,
  though some surrounding nations will be spared (v. 41).
- The antichrist "will extend his power" against other countries
  and be on the verge of a complete and overwhelming victory
  (vv. 42-43). Revelation 13 informs us he will rule the world for
  a time.

- He will become terrified as he receives "reports from the east and the north" (v. 44).
- He will again pursue his enemies "with great fury to annihilate and completely destroy" (v. 44) them (cf. Rev 9:13-19; 16:12).
- He will set up camp in Israel, but with a mere whimper "he will meet his end with no one to help him" (v. 45). Turn out the lights. His show is over.

I again appreciate Stephen Miller's concluding words on all of this:

> Antichrist will meet these attacking forces in Palestine and make his headquarters ("pitch his royal tents") "between the seas at the beautiful holy mountain." "Seas" denotes the two bodies of water on either side of Israel, the Mediterranean Sea on the west and the Dead Sea on the east. The "beautiful holy mountain" is Mount Zion, where the temple stood, rendering the mountain "beautiful" and "holy." Antichrist will use the Jerusalem temple for his headquarters (cf. 2 Thess. 2:4; possible Matt. 24:15), though the brunt of the battle will be elsewhere. Daniel was here reporting that the final war will be fought in Israel, a fact set forth elsewhere in Scripture (cf. Ezek. 39:2-29; Joel 3:2-16; Zech. 12:2-9; 14:1-21). The Book of Revelation indicates more specifically that the valley of Megiddo will be the setting of this final conflict—the Battle of Armageddon (cf. Rev. 16:16).
>
> Finally, the career of the most evil man in history will be terminated. Earlier in the book Daniel revealed that "the little horn" will be judged when the Lord comes to set up his kingdom (7:1,26-27); Paul said this "man of lawlessness" will be destroyed "by the splendor of his [Christ's] coming" (2 Thess. 2:8); and John teaches that the "beast" will be captured and thrown into the lake of fire at Christ's return (Rev. 19:20). This chapter closes with the pronouncement that there will be no escape (no "help" from any source) for Antichrist when the judgment of God falls upon him and his evil empire. (*Daniel*, 312)

This puny human despot meets the King of kings and the Lord of lords (Rev 19:11-21). It is no contest!

Conclusion: How Does This Text Point to Christ?

The Lord Jesus is so easily seen in this text by way of contrast with both Antiochus and the antichrist. His goodness in opposition to their evilness is a bright and radiant light that shines with the glory of God on full display. A simple comparative chart makes plain what we have in the Son of Man of Daniel 7, the anointed ruler of Daniel 9.

Antiochus/Antichrist	King Jesus
Despised (11:20)	Desired
Deceitful (11:23)	Truthful
Hates the holy covenant (11:28)	Loves God's holy covenant
Desecrates the temple (11:31)	Cleanses the temple
Abolished sacrifices (11:31)	Made sacrifice once for all
Persecutes and murders God's people (11:32-33)	Refines and purifies God's people
Willful (11:36)	Submissive
Exalts himself (11:36)	Humbles himself
Magnifies himself as god (11:36)	Incarnated himself as God
Blasphemes God (11:36)	Glorifies God
Worships the god of war (11:38)	Is the God of Peace
His kingdom will end (11:45)	His kingdom endures forever

Reflect and Discuss

1. How would you describe the "spirit of the antichrist" (1 John 4:3)? Where do you see this spirit at work today?
2. How have you previously thought about the coming of the antichrist? How does it fit with the prophecy of Daniel 11?
3. Review and restate in your own words the idea of prophetic foreshortening. Does this feature mean these parts of the Bible are not true? Explain.
4. What are the tools Antiochus uses to achieve his evil goals? How might you be tempted to use these same means in your own life?
5. Read Luke 6:43-45 and James 1:13-15. What do these verses say about the source of our sin?

6. How does God use difficulty to work in his people in Daniel 11? How has he used difficulty to work in your own life?
7. What marks the faithful believers in Daniel 11? How can you imitate their faithfulness to the Lord in your setting?
8. What are the defining characteristics of the antichrist, the man?
9. How does the image of the antichrist contrast with the image of Jesus as presented in Revelation?
10. What comfort should God's people receive from such a horrible portrait of the antichrist? Why would this prophecy be helpful for God's people?

Nine Marks of Eschatological Discipleship

DANIEL 12:1-13

Main Idea: In light of God's sovereign control over history and the promised return of Christ, God's people must pursue faithfulness and fruitfulness all the way to the end.

I.   Be Comforted by God's Protection (12:1).
II. Be Ready for Trouble and Intense Persecution (12:1,7).
III. Count on God to Rescue His People (12:1).
IV. Hope in the Resurrection (12:2).
V.   Live Wisely and Point Others to Jesus (12:3).
VI. Treasure God's Word and Grow in Your Understanding of It (12:4).
VII. Patiently Trust That God Will End Things at the Right Time (12:5-9).
VIII. Pursue Holiness and Rejoice in Its Fruits (12:10).
IX. Endure to the End, Knowing It Is Worth It (12:11-13).

In 1 John 3:2, the apostle makes a wonderful *declaration* concerning our future:

> *Dear friends, we are God's children now, and what we will be has not yet been revealed. We know that when he appears, we will be like him because we will see him as he is.*

John then follows up in verse 3 with a clear *application*: "And everyone who has this hope in him purifies himself just as he is pure." John's point is clear: Future destiny impacts present discipleship. What I will be someday will mold and shape how I live today.

The prophet Daniel conveyed that same message in the final chapter of his prophetic masterpiece. The hope of my future resurrected body (12:2) provides motivation for discipleship (v. 3) and personal holiness (v. 10). In fact, it seems to me we can identify no fewer than nine marks of what I am calling "eschatological discipleship" in Daniel 12. More specifically, Daniel 12 teaches us how to live as faithful exiles in a world, a context, that is not our home. It helps us answer the question, How can we live as kingdom citizens, dedicated disciples, in a land that is strange and even hostile toward us?

The vision that began in 11:2 actually continues through 12:4. Verses 5-13 then serve as the epilogue or conclusion. Still, clear continuity links 12:1-4 with 12:5-13. I recently read that

> the Old Testament book in which the exiled Daniel refuses to obey orders to worship the king rather than his own god [sic] is seen as "very dangerous" by the Chinese government in light of the explosion of Christianity in China. (Phillips, "China on Course to Become 'World's Most Christian Nation' within 15 Years")

I can understand that, and chapter 12 is a fitting finale to this guide for exile living, as it provides what Sinclair Ferguson calls "the eschatological ethic that characterizes all Scripture" (*Daniel*, 223). So what are the nine marks of eschatological discipleship the last chapter of Daniel provides?

Be Comforted by God's Protection
DANIEL 12:1

Chapter 12 begins with "At that time," which links 12:1 with 11:36-45 and the reign and end of the antichrist. When that eschatological day arrives, God will raise up the angel Michael (cf. 10:13,21), who is identified as "the great prince who stands watch over your people." Michael is called the archangel in Jude 9. He leads a victorious war against Satan and his angels (demons) in Revelation 12:7-12. Michael is, as are all angels, a ministering spirit "sent out to serve those who are going to inherit salvation" (Heb 1:14). He no doubt is ministering to God's people today, but at the "time of distress" (Dan 12:1) or "the time of the end" (12:4,9,13) he will intensify his involvement on behalf of the people of God. To Daniel and his readers, I believe this referred to the righteous remnant of Israel, "the holy people" (12:7). Looking at it from this side of Pentecost and with the insights of Romans 11 and Ephesians 3, we know it points to the church, the eschatological community of the redeemed of all ages. God takes a particular interest in his holy people purchased by the blood of his Son.

Dale Davis puts it well:

> From Daniel 10 we understand Michael to be the warrior-advocate of Israel who takes up the cudgels on their behalf.

There are unseen legions (cf. Matt. 26:53; Heb. 1:14) standing behind the wobbly people of God in their darkest trouble. (*Message of Daniel*, 162)

So be comforted by God's protection as you live for Jesus. His angels are on your side, and they are busy at work on your behalf.

Be Ready for Trouble and Intense Persecution
DANIEL 12:1,7

Second Timothy 3:12 reminds us that "all who want to live a godly life in Christ Jesus will be persecuted." This basic theological axiom runs true throughout redemptive history in both testaments. But as history as we know it draws to a close, opposition, persecution, and suffering will escalate so that "there will be a time of distress such as never has occurred since nations came into being until that time" (Dan 12:1). Verse 7 adds that this will be "when the power of the holy people is shattered." This will be when "all these things will be completed."

This time of distress or trouble echoes Jeremiah 30:7 and the time of Jacob's trouble. It also is found on the lips of the Lord Jesus in Mark 13:19 (cf. Matt 24:21-22). Trouble is on the way. It comes now, of course, in the regular ebb and flow of normal life in a broken and fallen world. Such troubles, however, are only an inkling, a foretaste, of what will come at the time of the end. Since we have no idea when that day will be, we must prepare ourselves in the present. Living as a holy people, even if we are shattered, broken in pieces, must be a vital part of our discipleship. Purifying ourselves, cleansing ourselves, being refined by the power of the gospel and the Holy Spirit will not be an optional consideration. It will be essential warfare equipment for the battles we engage. It will not be a small skirmish. It will be a take-no-prisoners total war! The brilliant philosopher of science and mathematics John Lennox simply notes,

It is hard to get one's mind around this grim statement. The time of Antiochus was horrendous, as was the period around the later fall of Jerusalem. The Holocaust beggars description. But Daniel indicates that there is even worse to come at the time of the end. (*Against the Flow*, 341)

Be prepared. Be ready. Don't get caught by surprise.

Count on God to Rescue His People
DANIEL 12:1

A time of unprecedented trouble is coming for God's people. However, don't be alarmed. Gabriel promises Daniel, "At that time your people shall be delivered" (ESV). And who are Daniel's people? They are "everyone whose name shall be written in the book" (ESV). This is a reference to the book of life (cf. Rev 20:12,15), the Lamb's book of life (cf. Rev 13:8; 21:27). It also is an echo of Psalm 69:28 and a precious promise for the people of God. The antichrist may rage against the holy people of God. It may seem for a while like he will succeed and be victorious. Saints will suffer, and saints will die (as they are all around the world today). But do not panic. Don't be afraid. Deliverance is on the way, as Daniel 7 promised with the glorious coming of the Son of Man, the Lord Jesus Christ.

Further, be comforted. Your deliverance is assured because your name is written in the book! Your eternal destiny is secure. Your heavenly citizenship cannot be revoked. The book of life contains your name and is a guarantee of final and certain salvation. H. C. Leupold puts it beautifully:

> That a record of heaven with reference to those who are to inherit eternal life should be available is equivalent to saying that God's thoughts for the salvation for his children run back into eternity, and that He loves to busy Himself with their eternal welfare. (*Exposition of Daniel*, 528–29)

You can count on God to rescue his people.

Hope in the Resurrection
DANIEL 12:2

One component of God's deliverance is our future bodily resurrection. The empty tomb of Jesus Christ in Jerusalem is our guarantee. Verse 2 discusses this future hope in terms of a general resurrection, drawing a contrast between the righteous (v. 3) and the unrighteous. Resurrection day will also be separation day.

Drawing from the language of Genesis 3:19 and the curse of sin warranting our death both physically and spiritually, God's Word promises that those whose bodies lie in the grave will be reanimated by the power of God with no exceptions. All will be bodily raised. However, at that point the similarities end. Some will awake to everlasting life because their names are "found written in the book" (v. 1). Others, tragically, will awake and rise "to disgrace and eternal contempt" (Dan 12:2) only to be cast into the lake of fire (Rev 20:14-15) where, as Revelation 14:11 says, "the smoke of their torment goes up forever and ever, and they have no rest, day or night" (ESV).

C. S. Lewis, in sobering terms, helps us understand what is at stake according to this verse, as well as our proper response:

> It is a serious thing to live in a society of possible gods and goddesses, to remember that the dullest and most uninteresting person you talk to may one day be a creature which, if you saw it now, you would be strongly tempted to worship, or else a horror and a corruption such as you now meet, if at all, only in a nightmare. All day long we are, in some degree, helping each other to one or the other of these destinations. . . . There are no *ordinary* people. You have never talked to a mere mortal. . . . It is immortals whom we joke with, work with, marry, snub, and exploit—immortal horrors or everlasting splendours. (*The Weight of Glory,* 45–46, emphasis in original)

God's people have hope in their future bodily resurrection.

Live Wisely and Point Others to Jesus
DANIEL 12:3

Verse 3 could be called "a soul-winner's promise" (cf. Ps 126:5-6). It is an appropriate companion to the wonderful promise and striking truth of verse 2. The insightful (cf. 11:33) are busy about the business of disciple-making (to use the language of the New Testament). They encourage others to turn to God. Those who

> influence others to go on walking in righteousness and assist them in remaining faithful in the pressure of the times will "shine like the brightness of the sky above . . . like the stars forever and ever." (Davis, *Message of Daniel,* 162)

Bob Fyall says this verse "is a powerful motive for evangelism" (*Daniel,* 188). John Calvin adds,

No one of God's children ought to confine their attention privately to themselves, but as far as possible, everyone ought to interest himself in the welfare of his brethren. God has deposited the teaching of his salvation with us, not for the purpose of our privately keeping it to ourselves, but of our pointing out the way of salvation to all mankind. (*Commentaries on the Book of Daniel*, 376–77)

I love the simple paraphrase of Eugene Peterson in *The Message*: "Those who put others on the right path to life will glow like stars forever." Do you want to be an all-star for King Jesus? Then do the work of a soul-winner following in the footsteps of the Savior (Luke 19:10).

Treasure God's Word and Grow in Your Understanding of It
DANIEL 12:4

Verse 4 is a bit tricky and susceptible to misunderstanding. Daniel, interestingly and surprisingly, is told to "keep these words secret and seal the book until the time of the end." The idea is not to hide the words but to protect them, keeping them safe. Joyce Baldwin notes, "'Seal the book' has the double sense of authenticating and of preserving intact (cf. Is. 8:16; Je. 32:11,14)" (*Daniel*, 206). God's people need this word from our Lord, especially as we move toward the end of the age. We need to be ready and not taken by surprise. The closer we get to the end, the more important God's Word and the understanding of it will be.

The last phrase of verse 4 is enigmatic: "Many will roam about, and knowledge will increase." Some read it negatively, referring to unbelievers and drawing a parallel to Amos 8:12 (Ferguson, *Daniel*, 227). Because of the near context of verse 3, however, I cautiously take it in a positive sense. Dale Davis explains,

As the Lord's people give diligent attention to this piece of Scripture, they will, especially nearer the end, have a clearer grasp of its meaning. . . . It is immersion that brings insight. (*Message of Daniel*, 164)

Stephen Miller puts it clearly and simply:

As the time of fulfillment draws nearer, the "wise" will seek to comprehend these prophecies more precisely, and God will grant understanding ("knowledge") to them. (*Daniel*, 321)

Patiently Trust That God Will End Things at the Right Time
DANIEL 12:5-9

In verses 5-9 the vision shifts as two other angels join Gabriel, who has been talking to Daniel. They stand opposite each other on the banks of the Tigris River (cf. 10:4). Next, "the man dressed in linen" (cf. 10:5-6) appears again "above the water of the river" (12:6). This is the glorified Son of God, robed in his priestly purity. One of the angels asks him, "How long until the end of these wondrous things?" (ESV, "wonders"; NIV, "astonishing things"). How long will these extraordinary things continue once they start? When will they stop? There is an urgency to the request. Further, this is a question to which even the angels do not know the answer. Jesus reaffirms this in Mark 13:32.

In a display of amazing solemnity and seriousness, the Son of God raises both hands to heaven (cf. Gen 14:22; Deut 32:40), an unusual act, and he invokes an oath "by him who lives eternally" (12:7). The answer to the angel's question is twofold: (1) "It would be for a time, times, and half a time" or three and a half years; (2) This terrible and intense "time of distress" (12:1) will end right on time, according to God's timetable, "when the power of the holy people is shattered." It is then and only then that "all these things will be completed." Ligon Duncan puts it well:

> When evil has done its worst, we are told, as soon as [it
> finishes] shattering the power of the holy people, all these
> events will be complete. When evil has done its worst and the
> hopes of the people of God seem shattered, then God will act.
> The grim work of the oppressors will roll on and on and on.
> But at the appropriate moment God will intervene. ("Blessed
> Is the One Who Waits")

Daniel's response in verse 8 so encourages me: "I heard but did not understand." I can certainly identify with that. So he follows up with a question of his own, "My lord, what will be the outcome of these things?" Verse 9 gives him his answer, but probably not the one he wanted. Respectfully Daniel is told, "Go on your way, Daniel, for the words are secret and sealed until the time of the end." Go on about your life and business, Daniel. You have received all you are going to get, and it is enough. This prophecy and its understanding will become more clear only "as God unravels history in the unseen future" (Ferguson, *Daniel*, 229). The word is protected, and it will be preserved. Everything will happen as God intends at the right time. Be faithful. Trust him. Be patient. As Adrian Rogers so often said, "God is never late, and he is never early. He is always right on time!"

Pursue Holiness and Rejoice in Its Fruits
DANIEL 12:10

When it comes to eschatology, there are things we know and things we don't know and can't know because God has chosen not to reveal them to us. However, one thing we can know with certainty is how we are to live in light of the Son of Man's coming at the time of the end. And there is good news. God will see to it that the things related to our redemption come to pass. In those days of great distress and trouble God will see to it that his "holy people" (12:7), his bright and shining ones (v. 3), those whom he will raise to "everlasting life" (v. 2 ESV), "will be purified, cleansed, and refined" (v. 10).

In contrast, God's enemies will only be hardened in their sin and rebellion against his sovereign authority. Dale Davis says it well:

> The wicked will—what else—*act wickedly*. . . . *None of the wicked will understand* [cf. Rom. 1:22], *but only the wise will come to understand*. . . . The wicked remain in their accustomed darkness, but the Lord's wise ones will discern the issues of the time, what they are called to do and what it will cost them. Their "understanding" may also include having more exact clarity about the meaning of the revelation given via Daniel's "book." (*Message of Daniel*, 166, emphasis in original)

Endure to the End, Knowing It Is Worth It
DANIEL 12:11-13

I love the honesty and humility of James Boice when it comes to these verses. Concerning them he simply says that there are things here "which we cannot yet explain" (*Daniel*, 122). Acknowledging that exact sentiment, I will give it my best, knowing caution is the wisest course to take.

Once again we have a reference to "the abomination of desolation" (v. 11; cf. 9:27; 11:31; Matt 24:15; also 2 Thess 2:3-4). Dale Davis again is helpful when he says,

Verse 11 is speaking of the repression of true worship (*the regular offering . . . taken away*) and the imposition of false worship (*an appalling abomination . . .* put in place). We have already noted that Antiochus Epiphanes would do this sort of thing (8:11-13 and 11:31), yet there will be another near the end who will out-Antiochus Antiochus, one who will not only put a stop to legitimate worship (9:27b) but along with "abominations" is himself one "who makes desolate" or "is causing horror" (9:27c); now in 12:11, under the aegis of this "final scourge" of history, the *abomination making desolate* appears again. I think Jesus has 9:27 and 12:11 in view when he refers to the "abomination of desolation" in Mark 13:14. Even though "abomination" in that text is a neuter noun, the following participle is masculine—"where *he* ought not" (emphasis mine). Jesus agrees with Daniel 9:27 that the "abomination" is supremely a person and assumes that his appearance is future to Jesus' own earthly ministry. (*Message of Daniel,* 166–67)

This seems to me to be a reasonable and persuasive interpretation. But what of the 1,290 days of verse 11, and the beatitude of verse 13: "Happy is the one who waits for and reaches 1,335 days"? With James Boice, here I must confess my lack of understanding. This much, I believe, we can say: our Lord promises to bless those who endure and persevere through these difficult and troubling times of opposition and persecution. These specific numbers affirm God's sovereign control over the details of history. Things will move ahead as he has decreed, and things will also end as he has decreed. There is wonderful hope and assurance even if there remains mystery concerning the particularities.

The book concludes with a personal word for Daniel that can aid us all: "Go on your way to the end." You are in your last years, God says, but I still have work for you to do. When it is time for you to retire from my work, then I will bring you home. Then "you will rest" because you will be with me. Then, as promised in verse 2, you will "stand to receive your allotted inheritance" (v. 13; ESV, "allotted place"), your destiny, your reward. This will happen "at the end of the days." So do your duty, make disciples, proclaim my Word, and endure. Something wonderful is on the horizon at the end.

Conclusion: How Does This Text Point to Christ?

Just as we saw in Daniel 10:5-6, again we see the majestic man "dressed in linen" sovereignly standing above the earth and declaring his absolute authority over all things (12:7). This is a Christophany, a preincarnate appearance of the Second Person of the triune God. Both in appearance and action he conveys God's glory and greatness. He is Lord of history, not these petty tyrants, including the antichrist, who come and go. We must never forget and always "know that the Most High is ruler over human kingdoms. He gives [them] to anyone he wants and sets the lowliest of men over [them]" (4:17). Will we exalt the arrogant and prideful antichrist? Never! Will we exalt the humble Galilean from Nazareth? Absolutely!

Reflect and Discuss

1. What aspects of your discipleship need to be more fully shaped by your future destiny? How?
2. How does God protect his people? How have you experienced the protection of God?
3. Why is preparation for persecution a necessary part of discipleship? What kinds of persecution might you face for the sake of Christ?
4. Why can one's heavenly citizenship not be revoked? What comfort does this bring?
5. Why is the resurrection an important and necessary component of the gospel? Why do you think it is so often overlooked?
6. According to verse 3, what is the proper task of God's people living before "the end of the days"?
7. It is a basic principle of discipleship to study and meditate on God's Word. How can you, like Daniel, work to preserve and live according to God's revelation?
8. Do you ever grow impatient waiting for Christ's return? To what area of faithfulness is God calling you as you wait?
9. If salvation is secure in Christ, why does the Bible focus on God's people living holy lives?
10. Daniel ends with a call for endurance to the end. What other passages of Scripture call believers to persevere?

WORKS CITED

Baldwin, Joyce G. *Daniel: An Introduction and Commentary*. Tyndale Old Testament Commentary 21. Downers Grove, IL: InterVarsity, 1978.

Beckwith, Carl L., ed. *Ezekiel, Daniel*. Reformation Commentary on Scripture 12. Downers Grove, IL: IVP Academic, 2012.

Begg, Alistair. "Gabriel and the 70 Weeks." *TruthforLife.org*. November 8, 2015. https://www.truthforlife.org/resources/sermon/gabriel-and -70-weeks.

Belz, Joel. "Dare to Be a Daniel." *World*. March 30, 1996. http://www.world mag.com/1996/03/dare_to_be_a_daniel (no longer available online).

Boice, James Montgomery. *Daniel: An Expositional Commentary*. Grand Rapids, MI: Baker, 2003.

Bush, Russell. *A Handbook for Christian Philosophy*. Grand Rapids, MI: Zondervan, 1991.

Calvin, John. *Commentaries on the Book of Daniel*. Translated by Thomas Myers. Reprint. Calvin's Commentaries, vol. 13. Grand Rapids, MI: Baker, 2009.

Chapell, Bryan. *The Gospel According to Daniel: A Christ-Centered Approach*. Grand Rapids, MI: Baker, 2014.

Criswell, W. A., ed. *The Believer's Study Bible: New King James Version*. Nashville, TN: Thomas Nelson, 1991.

Davis, Dale Ralph. *The Message of Daniel: His Kingdom Cannot Fail*. Downers Grove, IL: InterVarsity, 2013.

Dorsey, David A. *The Literary Structure of the Old Testament: A Commentary on Genesis-Malachi*. Grand Rapids, MI: Baker, 1999.

Duncan, Dan. "Daniel." Believers Chapel Dallas. http://believerschapel dallas.org/sermons/old-testament/daniel-dd#top (no longer available online).

Duncan, Ligon. "Blessed Is the One Who Waits." *LigonDuncan.com*. March 29, 1998. http://ligonduncan.com/blessed-is-the-one-who -waits-878.

————. "Daniel in the Lion's Den." *LigonDuncan.com.* January 18, 1998. http://ligonduncan.com/daniel-in-the-lions-den-866.

————. "God and Monsters." http://believerschapel-production.s3 .amazonaws.com/dan_duncan/daniel/07_dd_daniel.pdf.

————. "The Handwriting on the Wall." *LigonDuncan.com.* January 11, 1998. http://ligonduncan.com/the-handwriting-on-the-wall-864.

————. "The Vision of the Man." *LigonDuncan.com.* March 15, 1998. http://ligonduncan.com/the-vision-of-the-man-875.

Edwards, Jonathan. "Some Thoughts Concerning the Revival." In *The Great Awakening,* vol. 4 of *The Works of Jonathan Edwards.* Edited by C. C. Goen. New Haven, CT: Yale University Press, 1970.

Ferguson, Sinclair B. *Daniel.* The Preacher's Commentary 21. Nashville, TN: Thomas Nelson, 1988.

Fyall, Robert S. *Daniel: A Tale of Two Cities.* Fearn, Ross-shire, Great Britain: Christian Focus, 1998.

Gangel, Kenneth O. *Daniel.* Holman Old Testament Commentary 18. Nashville, TN: B&H, 2001.

Greidanus, Sidney. *Preaching Christ from Daniel: Foundations for Expository Sermons.* Grand Rapids, MI: Eerdmans, 2012.

Gundry, Robert H. *The Church and the Tribulation.* Grand Rapids, MI: Zondervan, 1973.

Hartman, Louis Francis, and Alexander A. Di Lella. *The Book of Daniel.* The Anchor Bible 23. Garden City, NY: Doubleday, 1978.

Helm, David. *Daniel for You.* Purcellville, VA: The Good Book Company, 2015.

Hill, Andrew E. "Daniel," in *Daniel-Malachi.* Edited by Tremper Longman III and David E. Garland. Expositor's Bible Commentary 8. Rev. ed. Grand Rapids, MI: Zondervan, 2009.

The Holy Bible: English Standard Version: The ESV Study Bible. Wheaton, IL: Crossway Bibles, 2008.

Jackson, David. "Obama: Don't Use Religion to Deny Constitutional Rights," *USA Today.* September 28, 2015. http://www.usatoday.com /story/theoval/2015/09/28/obama-lgbt-democratic-party-kim -davis-gay-marriage-licenses/72959988.

Jeremiah, David. *Agents of Babylon: What the Prophecies of Daniel Tell Us about the End of Days.* Carol Stream, IL: Tyndale, 2015.

Keller, Tim. "What Is Gospel-Centered Ministry?" A presentation to the 2007 Gospel Coalition National Conference. http://resources .thegospelcoalition.org/library/what-is-gospel-centered-ministry-en.

Lennox, John C. *Against the Flow: The Inspiration of Daniel in an Age of Relativism.* Oxford: Monarch, 2015.

Leupold, H. C. *Exposition of Daniel.* Grand Rapids, MI: Baker, 1969.

Lewis, C. S. *Mere Christianity.* San Francisco, CA: HarperSanFrancisco, 2001.

———. *The Weight of Glory and Other Addresses.* San Francisco, CA: HarperSanFrancisco, 2000.

Longman, Tremper, III. *Daniel.* NIV Application Commentary. Grand Rapids, MI: Zondervan, 1999.

Lucas, Ernest. *Daniel.* Downers Grove, IL: InterVarsity, 2002.

MacArthur, John. *An Uncompromising Life.* Chicago, IL: Moody, 1988.

Miller, Stephen R. *Daniel.* New American Commentary 18. Nashville, TN: B&H, 1994.

Newell, Marvin J., ed. *Expect Great Things: Mission Quotes That Inform and Inspire.* Pasadena, CA: William Carey Library, 2013.

Olasky, Marvin. "Dare to Be a Daniel." *World.* September 15, 2015, 64.

Olthuis, James H. "On Worldviews." *Christians Scholar's Review* 15, no. 2 (1985): 153–64.

Péter-Contesse, René, and John Ellington. *A Handbook on the Book of Daniel.* New York, NY: United Bible Societies, 1993.

Phillips, Tom. "China on Course to Become 'World's Most Christian Nation' within 15 Years." *The Telegraph.* April 19, 2014. http://www.telegraph.co.uk/news/worldnews/asia/china/10776023/China-on-course-to-become-worlds-most-Christian-nation-within-15-years.html.

Pierce, Ronald W. *Daniel.* Teach the Text Commentary Series. Grand Rapids, MI: Baker, 2015.

Piper, John. "Angels and Prayer." *DesiringGod.org.* January 12, 1992. http://www.desiringgod.org/messages/angels-and-prayer.

———. "Believing God on Election Day." *DesiringGod.org.* November 6, 1988. http://www.desiringgod.org/messages/believing-god-on-election-day.

———. "Daniel's Defiance of Darius in Prayer." *DesiringGod.org.* December 29, 1991. http://www.desiringgod.org/messages/daniels-defiance-of-darius-in-prayer.

———. "How to Pray for a Desolate Church." *DesiringGod.org.* January 5, 1992. http://www.desiringgod.org/messages/how-to-pray-for-a-desolate-church.

Sire, James W. *The Universe Next Door: A Basic Worldview Catalogue.* Exp. ed. Downers Grove, IL: InterVarsity, 1988.

Smietana, Bob. "Pastors: The End of the World Is Complicated." *LifeWay NewsRoom*. April 26, 2016. http://blog.lifeway.com/newsroom /2016/04/26/pastors-the-end-of-the-world-is-complicated.

Spurgeon, C. H. *C. H. Spurgeon's Sermons on the Book of Daniel*. Edited by Charles Thomas Cook. Grand Rapids, MI: Zondervan, 1966.

Steinmann, Andrew. *Daniel*. Saint Louis, MO: Concordia, 2008.

Swindoll, Charles R. *Daniel: God's Pattern for the Future*. Fullerton, CA: Insight for Living, 1986.

Wagner, C. Peter. *Engaging the Enemy: How to Fight and Defeat Territorial Spirits*. Ventura, CA: Regal, 1991.

Walvoord, John F. *Daniel: The Key to Prophetic Revelation*. Chicago, IL: Moody, 1971.

Young, Edward J. *The Prophecy of Daniel: A Commentary*. Grand Rapids, MI: Eerdmans, 1949.

SCRIPTURE INDEX